7.50

Terminology
for Accountants

revised edition

The Canadian Institute of Chartered Accountants

© Copyright 1976
The Canadian Institute of Chartered Accountants
250 Bloor Street East
Toronto, Canada M4W 1G5

ISBN #0-88800-002-2

Printed and bound in Canada

Foreword

The ready acceptance and strong demand for previous editions of *Terminology for Accountants* have left little doubt as to the need for such a book. This need exists not only among accountants in practice, in industry, in government and in schools and universities, but also among non-accountants. This book should be of particular value to non-financial managers who have become increasingly aware in recent years of the importance of understanding the language of financial reporting.

As with any dictionary or permanent source of reference, *Terminology for Accountants, revised edition* is, in a sense, out-of-date as soon as it is printed. This is even more so today than when the earlier editions were published, so rapid are current developments in accounting thought and techniques. Nevertheless, at each stage in any development, it is important to establish a platform before taking the next step. Hence the value of this book today to accountants and non-accountants in the worlds of business, government and research.

The first Study of accounting terminology by the CICA, "Accounting Terminology for Canadian Practice", was published in 1938 and consisted of nearly 500 items. Over the years, the work has been revised and expanded. "Accounting Terminology" was published in 1957 with 517 terms and "Terminology for Accountants" in 1962 with 804. The present edition contains 1336 terms.

Terminology for Accountants, revised edition, was prepared by a Study Group, the names of the members of which are set out below. A French version of this publication, *Dictionnaire de la comptabilité,* has been prepared by Fernand Sylvain, CA, of Laval University. This includes additional terms in order to provide the correct French expression for a number of common English usage or common business terms for which an English definition was not necessary. A booklet of French-English/English-French equivalents, derived from this work, is available separately.

The Research Department is greatly indebted to the members of the Study Group for their participation and input and for their thoroughness and diligence. Particular thanks are due to André Desrochers, CA, Lorne J. Reesor, FCA, and Grace Lew, Research Assistant, for their valuable contributions. Many others provided helpful comments on various drafts and special thanks go to Christina S. R. Hutchins, CA, Murray M. Hahn, CA, H. Purdy Crawford, QC, and William R. Langdon, RIA, who reviewed terms in certain areas.

Toronto
May 1976

John H. Denman,
Research Studies Director

Study Group

P. H. Lyons, FCA, *Chairman*
Deloitte, Haskins & Sells,
Toronto, Ontario.

D. H. Bonham, FCA,
Queen's University,
Kingston, Ontario.

André Desrochers, CA,
Order of Chartered
    Accountants of Québec,
Montreal, Quebec.

S. J. Deudney, CA,
Canadian Depository for
    Securities Ltd.,
Toronto, Ontario.

C. S. R. Hutchins, CA,
Price Waterhouse & Co.,
Toronto, Ontario.

R. H. Kidd, CA,
Thorne Riddell & Co.,
Toronto, Ontario.

F. I. McNeil, CA,
Statistics Canada,
Ottawa, Ontario.

J. R. Rathwell, FCA,
G. H. Ward & Partners,
Lindsay, Ontario.

L. J. Reesor, FCA,
Price Waterhouse & Co.,
Toronto, Ontario.

M. S. Shapiro, FCA,
Toronto, Ontario.

J. E. Smyth, FCA,
University of Toronto,
Toronto, Ontario.

Preface

Terminology for Accountants, revised edition, is a revision and expansion of the edition published in 1962. Terms and definitions in that edition have been reviewed; some of the entries have been carried forward with little or no change while others have been eliminated or substantially revised to reflect current usage. New terms, both those which have come into common use and those which were passed over in the previous edition, have been added.

It is not the purpose of this book to dictate usage but rather to define and explain words and phrases which, through continued use, have become an accepted part of an accountant's vocabulary. The terms included are defined with the meanings encountered in general use; of course, in certain circumstances, the terms may have other special meanings or alternative definitions such as those used in the context of a specific statute or part of the *CICA Handbook.*

Because this book is designed as a dictionary and is concerned with the use of words or phrases, extensive information on the subjects suggested by those words and phrases has not been provided, nor have computation methods been covered. For example, this book contains a broad definition of *earnings per share* but anyone wanting to know how to compute earnings per share would have to refer to the *Handbook.*

The terms included are in general use by accountants but are not necessarily limited to accounting. Although everyday words which have acquired a special meaning for accountants have been included, common English usage or common business usage terms which have little or no special meaning for accountants have not.

New terms and definitions are constantly knocking at the door of the accountant's word house. Some of them are admitted and some of them are not and this has been reflected in this book. One of the neologisms that has not yet managed to achieve standing in the accountant's dictionary is FISH, the abbreviation for the cost allocation method first in, still here.

Accountants use terms from other disciplines such as statistics and mathematics, computers and data processing, tax and economics. This book includes few of these terms because there are dictionaries and glossaries available (as for example those in the CICA publications *Computer Control Guidelines* and *Computer Audit Guidelines*) which deal more comprehensively with these terms.

Of those words and phrases that might be considered to be primarily legal or economic in their connotations, only the terms that have a specialized usage among accountants are included and, usually, only the special meanings are given. A few tax terms are included to distinguish them from related accounting definitions; no attempt is made to provide technically precise definitions for any tax terms.

Where more than one meaning is given to a particular word or phrase, the alternative definitions are presented in preferential order so far as possible. Synonyms are cross-referenced to one definition, usually placed under the preferred term.

Generic groups of words have been brought together with convenience and facility of reference deciding the groupings. Each term in the generic group is also listed in its normal alphabetical position with a cross-reference to the generic group.

The task of revising a work such as this is never done. Future revisions are inevitable and desirable. Suggestions for additions and improvements for the next edition would be welcomed and should be sent to the CICA Research Department.

P. H. Lyons, FCA,
Chairman,
Study Group on Revision of
Terminology for Accountants

Toronto
May 1976

Abbreviations used

abbr.	abbreviation
adj.	adjective
Br.	British
colloq.	colloquial
e.g.	for example
n.	noun
obs.	obsolete
pl.	plural
q.v.	which see
syn.	synonym
v.	verb
v.i.	intransitive verb
v.t.	transitive verb
U.S.	United States

A

abatement

1. The reduction of an expenditure. 2. The deduction of minor revenues incidental to an operation in calculating the cost of the operation. 3. A tax reduction provided for under statute.

absorbed burden

See **overhead.**

absorption costing

See **cost accounting method.**

acceptance

1. The written statement on a bill of exchange signed by the person on whom the bill is drawn (i.e. the person to whom the bill has been addressed), indicating his assent to the order of the drawer. 2. A bill of exchange that has been accepted.

access

The ability to obtain data from, or place data in, computer storage.

random access

Access to computer storage where information can be obtained directly regardless of its storage location.

sequential access

Access to computer storage that requires processing in turn of non-desired storage locations.

accommodation paper

A bill of exchange which has been signed by an accommodation party who thereby becomes liable on the bill to a holder for value.

accommodation party

A person who has signed a bill of exchange as drawer, acceptor or endorser, without receiving value therefor and for the purpose of assisting the person originally signing as drawer, acceptor or endorser.

account

n. 1. A formal record of an asset, liability, proprietorship, revenue, or expense, in which the effects of operations or transactions are indicated in terms of money or some other unit of measurement. 2. A statement setting out a summary of the operations or transactions in terms of money between individuals and/or organizations for a stated period. 3. (*pl.*)

Collective term for the whole set of financial statements of an organization, e.g. the annual accounts. 4. (*pl.*) Bookkeeping records in general. 5. (*obs.*) A financial statement.

v. (with *for*) 1. To keep accounts. 2. To render a statement of account.

account current
An account of mutual dealings and transactions between two persons, rendered by one to the other. Use of the term is generally limited to a statement of account between principal and agent, e.g. the statement of account rendered by a consignee to the consignor. (Compare **current account.**)

account form (of statement)
An arrangement of financial statement items in two columns with equal totals. See also **balance sheet, form of.** (Compare **report form.**)

account payable
An amount owing to a creditor. Generally limited to a liability for purchases of goods or services. In statement presentation, accounts payable may include open accounts and notes. See also **trade account payable.**

account receivable
An amount claimed against a debtor, usually arising from the sale of goods or services. In statement presentation, accounts receivable may include open accounts and notes. See also **trade account receivable.**

account sales
A statement rendered to a consignor of merchandise by the consignee giving particulars such as the sales of the consigned merchandise, amount of any such merchandise remaining unsold, gross proceeds, expenses incurred by the consignee, consignee's commission, and net amount due to the consignor.

accountancy
1. Accounting theory and practice as a whole. 2. The accounting profession.

accountant
1. A person skilled in accounting. 2. (*colloq.*) Often used to refer to **public accountant.**

accountant's comments
Syn. for **disclaimer.**

accounting
n. 1. The process of analyzing and systematically recording, in terms of money or some other unit of measurement, operations or transactions and of summarizing, reporting and interpreting the results thereof. (Compare **bookkeeping.**) 2. A formal report of the manner in which a responsibility has been discharged, e.g. an accounting by an agent to his principal or by an executor to the court.

accounting concepts
Syn. for **accounting postulates.**

accounting control
The accounting procedures used as a check on the reliability of the information contained in accounting records, e.g. the use of a control to balance the total of the accounts in a subsidiary ledger.

accounting conventions
A phrase of vague meaning encompassing accounting postulates, accounting principles and/or accounting procedures.

accounting cycle	The recurring process of opening books of account, recording all transactions during a period, preparation of financial statements and final closing of the books of account.
accounting deficiency	A failure to adhere to generally accepted accounting principles or to disclose essential information in financial statements. (Compare **auditing deficiency.**)
accounting engagement	A contract to perform certain specified accounting services for a client. See also **engagement letter.** (Compare **audit engagement.**)
accounting entity	One or more accounting units which are treated as one for purposes of financial reporting.
accounting income	The net income for the period shown in the financial statements prepared in accordance with generally accepted accounting principles for submission to shareholders. (Compare **taxable income.**)
accounting manual	A detailed description of the accounting policies followed by an organization, usually including an outline of the official procedures, forms, and responsibilities. (Compare **procedure manual.**)
accounting methods	Syn. for **accounting procedures.**
accounting period	That period of time for which financial statements are prepared, e.g. week, month, year.
accounting policies	The specific accounting principles followed by an organization and the procedures for applying those principles.
accounting postulates	The basic assumptions derived from observations of the economic and social environment, including the uses to which accounting information is put, which are pertinent to the development of accounting principles.
accounting practice	1. Syn. for **accounting procedures.** 2. See **practice.**
accounting principles	The rules which give guidance in the measurement, classification and interpretation of economic information and communication of the results through the medium of financial statements. These rules are characterized as "principles" by the fact that no alternative rule is generally recognized as permissible in the situation to which the principle relates.
accounting procedures	The methods, chosen from acceptable alternatives, followed by an organization in applying accounting principles.
accounting records	The books of account, and the supporting vouchers and other documentary evidence.
accounting system	The system used in an organization including procedures for recording, checking and reporting transactions.
accounting treatment	The accounting procedures used for recording or reporting a particular transaction or group of transactions.
accounting unit	An organization, or a department, section, or branch for which a separate set of accounts is maintained.

accretion	Growth as a result of natural causes (e.g. growth of timber) or increase by external additions (e.g. contributions to a pension fund.) (Compare **appreciation.**)
accrual basis of accounting	The method of recording transactions by which revenues and expenses are reflected in the accounts in the period in which they are considered to have been earned and incurred, respectively, whether or not such transactions have been finally settled by the receipt or payment of cash or its equivalent. (Compare **cash basis of accounting.**)
accrual method of tax allocation	See **tax allocation—interperiod tax allocation.**
accrue	*v.i.* 1. To increase, to be added as increase. 2. To come into existence as an enforceable claim or to vest as a right.
	v.t. In accounting usage, to record that which has accrued with the passage of time in connection with the rendering or receiving of service (e.g. interest, taxes, royalties, wages) but which is not yet an enforceable claim.
accrued asset	A developing but not yet enforceable claim against another person which is accumulating with the passage of time or the rendering of service. It arises from the sale of services (including the use of money) which at the date of accounting have been only partly performed, are not yet billable and have not been paid for.
accrued expense	An expense which has been incurred in an accounting period but for which no enforceable claim can be made in that accounting period by the person who rendered the service. It arises from the purchase of services (including the use of money) which at the date of accounting have been only partly performed, are not yet billable and have not been paid for.
accrued liability	A developing but not yet enforceable claim by another person, which is accumulating with the passage of time or the receipt of service. It arises from the purchase of services (including the use of money) which at the date of accounting have been only partly performed, are not yet billable and have not been paid for.
accrued revenue	Revenue which has been earned in an accounting period but for which no enforceable claim can be made in that accounting period against the person for whom the service was rendered. It arises from the sale of services (including the use of money) which at the date of accounting have been only partly performed, are not yet billable and have not been paid for.
accumulated depletion	The total to date of the periodic depletion charges on wasting assets since the assets were placed in use.
accumulated depreciation	The total to date of the periodic depreciation charges on fixed assets since the assets were placed in use.
accumulated earnings	Syn. for **surplus—retained earnings.**

accumulated tax allocation (debit/credit)	See **deferred income taxes.**
acid test ratio	See **ratio analysis.**
acquired share	See **share.**
acquisition	See **business combination.**
acquisition equation	An equation reflecting a business combination, in which the net assets brought into the combination represent one side of the equation and the consideration given represents the other side.
acquisition review	A review of the financial affairs of a company for the purpose of disclosing matters that may influence the terms or conclusion of a potential acquisition.
activity accounting	Syn. for **responsibility accounting.**
actuarial cost methods	Methods used by actuaries for allocating costs to particular periods. Such methods include computations involving compound interest, retirement and mortality estimates.
actuarial gains or losses	Changes in the actuarially calculated liability for certain costs (e.g. pension costs) as a result of changes in actuarial assumptions or deviations between actual experience and the assumptions used.
adjusting entry	1. An entry made before closing the books for the period, to apportion amounts of revenue or expense to accounting periods or to operating divisions. 2. A correcting entry.
administration expenses administrative expenses	Expenses of an organization relating to the overall direction of its affairs, as contrasted with expenses incurred for other specialized functions, such as manufacturing, selling or financing.
administrator	1. A person who manages the affairs of an organization. 2. A technical (legal) title given to a court-appointed person who manages the estate of a deceased person. (Compare **executor.**)
ad valorem	A method of levying a tax or duty on goods by using their estimated value as the tax base.
advance	*n.* 1. A payment that is to be accounted for by the recipient at some later date, e.g. payment for expenses to be incurred. 2. A payment made on account of, but before completion of, a contract, or before receipt of goods or services. 3. A loan.
adverse opinion	See **auditor's opinion.**
affairs, statement of	See **statement of affairs.**
affiliated company	1. A company which directly or indirectly, through one or more intermediaries, controls or is controlled by or is under common control with, another company. 2. Syn. for **associated company.** 3. A company related to another company in a manner defined by legislation for particular purposes.

agent

A person who acts on behalf of another person (the principal) by his authority, express or implied. (Compare **broker** 1.)

aging

A process of analysis of receivables by classifying the amounts according to the length of time for which they have been outstanding or for which they have been due. The time may be measured from the billing date or from the due date for each amount.

all-financial-resources concept

The view that a statement of changes in financial position is more informative and useful when it reports all additions of financial resources to the entity and all distribution of resources as well as changes in the composition of resources. See **statement of changes in financial position** and **statement of source and application of funds.**

all-inclusive income statement (form)

A form of financial statement presentation where all transactions affecting the net increase or decrease in owners' equity during the period, except capital transactions, are shown in the income statement. (Compare **current operating performance concept.**)

all-purpose financial statement

Syn. for **general purpose financial statement.**

allied company

Syn. for **associated company.**

allocate

1. To apportion or assign a debit or credit to appropriate accounts, e.g. to charge a rental payment to various departments depending on the floor space of the rented premises occupied by each. 2. (*government accounting*) To authorize a budgeted appropriation for a particular function.

allocation

The process or result of allocating. See also **tax allocation.**

allotment

1. In corporate accounting the acceptance of subscriptions for securities. 2. (*government accounting*) A sub-division of a budget appropriation which identifies the maximum amount authorized to be expended within a specified time period. It may be expressed in terms of objects of expenditure, activities or programs/projects.

allowance

1. A rebate or reduction in respect of a sale of goods or services, e.g. an allowance to compensate for damage to goods in transit or failure of goods to meet a specified quality. 2. A deduction from the book value of assets to reduce them to the estimated realizable value. 3. An amount paid to an employee or agent under an arrangement in respect of expenses. See also **expense account** 2. 4. (*colloq.*) A deduction from the book value of assets to indicate that portion of the value thereof that has been charged to expense.

alteration

A change in or a modification of a fixed asset.

amalgamation.

See **business combination.**

amortization
1. The gradual and systematic writing off of a balance in an account over an appropriate period. Depreciation accounting is a form of amortization applied to tangible fixed assets. Depletion accounting is another form of amortization applied to wasting assets. 2. The gradual extinction or provision for extinction of a debt by serial redemption or sinking fund payments.

amortized cost
The original cost of an asset less any portion amortized or treated as an expense or loss.

amortized value
The value at which an asset has been recorded in the books less any portion amortized or treated as an expense or loss.

analysis
The methodical investigation of a problem by resolving it into its simple components. See also **ratio analysis.**

   correlation analysis
The observation and measurement of the relationship, if any, between statistical series.

   cost/benefit analysis
The evaluation of the profits, income, output or other benefits anticipated under a project or service against the costs of obtaining them.

   cost/volume/profit analysis
The study of the effect on profits of changes in fixed costs, variable costs, sales quantities, sales prices and/or sales mix.

   incremental analysis
The evaluation of the changes in revenue and expenses that would result from a course of action.

   input/output analysis
The summary, in a square matrix, of the transactions between all economic units involved, which shows the resources consumed or utilized by an economic unit and the resulting product of that unit.

   network analysis
A method of planning and scheduling a project which uses a diagram consisting of geometrical figures to identify the interrelated sequences which must be accomplished to complete the project.

   regression analysis
The estimation of the value of one factor (the dependent variable) from the values of other factors (the independent variables), using statistical methods.

   sensitivity analysis
The study of the impact of a change in one variable on other variables and on the final results, using statistical methods.

analytical auditing
An auditing technique based upon appraisal of an organization's accounting systems and internal control, characterized by the use of flow charts, and limited but in-depth testing of transactions to determine the satisfactory operation of the systems.

annual report
The information provided annually by the directors or management of an organization, to the shareholders, owners, or other interested parties concerning operations and financial position. Usually, it includes the annual financial statements, the auditor's report thereon, and the reports of officers or directors.

annual return
annual summary

A statutory information return to be filed with a designated government department under certain laws such as the Canadian and provincial corporations acts.

annuity depreciation method   See **depreciation method.**

anti-dilution

In the calculation of fully diluted earnings per share, the effect of potential issues of additional common shares which would increase earnings per share or decrease a loss per share.

applied cost

A cost that has been assigned or apportioned to a product or activity.

applied overhead   See **overhead.**

apportionment

1. The division and allocation or distribution of an amount in proportionate parts. 2. (*executorship accounting*) The allocation of receipts and disbursements to income and corpus (capital), in order to determine the respective interests of life tenants and remaindermen.

appraisal

A valuation, especially of land, buildings, machinery, and equipment, made by individuals or firms qualified as expert in such valuations. The valuation may be made on one of several bases, e.g. replacement cost, replacement cost less observed depreciation, market value.

appraisal increase credit
appraisal increment

The credit resulting from an increase in the recorded value of fixed assets arising from an appraisal. A suitable designation for an appraisal increase would be "Excess of appraised value of fixed assets over cost" (or "over depreciated cost", if that is the case).

appraisal surplus   (*obs.*) Syn. for **appraisal increase credit.**

appreciation

Increase in value over cost or book value. Generally, the term refers to increases resulting from external influences such as rising prices rather than to increases resulting from utility added by action of the owner. (Compare **accretion**.)

appropriated retained earnings   See **surplus—retained earnings.**

appropriation

1. A transfer of net income or of retained earnings to a special account to restrict availability for distribution, e.g. a transfer of retained earnings to a reserve. 2. An authorization to make expenditures, usually limited in amount and time. 3. (*government accounting*) An approved budget estimate which represents the maximum amount of funds authorized to be expended but which does not by itself constitute authorization to make expenditures.

appropriation account

1. (*Br.*) An account to which net profits are carried and from which transfers are made to reflect the disposition of such profits. 2. An account for a budget estimate, especially in government accounting.

appropriation ledger	In budgetary accounting, especially for governments, a subsidiary ledger containing an account for each appropriation. Usually each account shows the original appropriation and subsequent transactions; encumbrances and expenditures; and unencumbered and unexpended balances.
arbitrage	The simultaneous purchase and sale of the identical securities, commodities or foreign currencies in different markets to profit from price discrepancies.
arm's length	*adj.* 1. A general term applied to any transaction where the parties to the transaction are not related or connected with each other. 2. Under income tax legislation, the term has a special meaning.
arrears of dividends	See **dividend** 1.
articles of association	The internal regulations of a limited company incorporated by registration; analogous to the by-laws of a limited company incorporated by letters patent. See **by-law** 2.
articles of incorporation	See **instrument of incorporation.**
asked price	See **bid/asked price.**
assessed value	See **assessment.**
assessment	The process of determining the amount of a tax levy or dues payable. In the case of a municipal real property tax, the assessment is the value for taxation purposes placed on the property to be taxed, an "assessment notice" informs the taxpayer of this valuation, while the notice of the amount of tax to be paid is usually called the "tax notice" or "tax bill". In the case of self-assessed taxes, such as income or corporation taxes, the notice sent to the taxpayer confirming or altering the amount of tax is called the "notice of assessment".
asset	1. In general, a thing of value owned. 2. In accounting, money or monetary equivalents (investments) or the expectation of future benefit arising from events and transactions prior to the accounting date, including claims on others for payment or service (receivables and prepaids), or the earned portion of future expected claims (accrued income), the expectation of future value through sale (inventories for sale), the expectation of future value through use (fixed assets, stocks of supplies), or a generalized expectation of future benefit from past expenditure (deferred charges).
assignment	A transfer of property, or of a right or interest in property, by one person to another to be used by the recipient for his own benefit or for the benefit of creditors or to be held in trust.
associated company **associated corporation**	1. A company operating either wholly or partially in co-operation with another by reason of common control, contract or agreement. (Compare **affiliated company** 1.) 2. A company related to another company in a manner defined by legislation for particular purposes.

attest function	The expression of a professional opinion on financial statements by a public accountant.
audit	*n.* 1. An examination of evidential matter to determine the reliability of a record or assertion. 2. In connection with financial statements, an examination of the accounting records and other supporting evidence of an organization for the purpose of expressing an opinion as to whether financial statements of the organization present fairly its position as at a given date and the results of its operations for the period ended on that date in accordance with generally accepted accounting principles.
analytical audit	See **analytical auditing.**
balance sheet audit	An audit sufficient to provide the basis for an expression of opinion as to whether the balance sheet presents a fair view of the financial position of the organization, usually without implying any extensive examination of the records of transactions for the period; an examination of position rather than transactions.
cash audit	An audit of cash transactions for a stated period. A cash audit is detailed in character but limited in scope. It is concerned with the accuracy of the records of cash receipts and disbursements, primarily to establish the balance of cash for which the persons charged with responsibility are accountable.
continuous audit	Any audit the various phases of which are performed continuously or at short intervals during the accounting period.
detailed audit	An audit in which a detailed examination is made of all or almost all entries and transactions. (Compare **test audit.**)
interim audit	Those phases of an audit which are conducted during the accounting period under review.
internal audit	An audit conducted by an employee or employees of the organization.
management audit	An examination of the effectiveness and efficiency of an enterprise's organizational structure, its policies and practices, its system and procedures and its use of human, financial and physical facilities.
operational audit	Syn. for **management audit.**
procedural audit	An examination of internal controls and other procedures of an organization for the purpose of assessing their efficiency and reliability.
statutory audit	An audit carried out under the provisions of a statute, such as a Corporations Act, *The Bank Act,* a Municipal Act.
test audit	An audit which is carried out by examining selected samples of transactions and accounting operations. (Compare **detailed audit.**)
year-end audit	Phases of an audit which are conducted at or after the end of the accounting period under review.

audit	*v.* To conduct an audit.
audit committee	A committee of directors of a corporation whose specific responsibility is to review the annual financial statements before submission to the board of directors. The committee generally acts as liaison between the auditor and the board of directors and its activities may include the review of nomination of the auditors, overall scope of the audit, results of the audit, internal financial controls and financial information for publication.
audit engagement	A contract of appointment as auditor of an organization. See also **engagement letter**. (Compare **accounting engagement**.)
audit evidence	Documents and other information that an auditor uses in forming his professional opinion.
audit program	A detailed listing of the nature and extent of procedures to be carried out in a particular audit engagement.
audit software	The computer programs and routines used to audit records maintained on electronic data processing equipment.
audit trail	The route by which the processing of data can be traced either forward or backward through the processing cycle.
auditing deficiency	The existence of limitations in the scope of an auditor's examination or his inability to obtain information essential for forming his opinion. (Compare **accounting deficiency**.)
auditing manual	Written instructions setting out auditing policies and procedures.
auditing practices	Syn. for **auditing procedures**.
auditing principles	Syn. for **auditing standards**.
auditing procedures	The steps carried out by an auditor to apply auditing techniques in particular circumstances.
auditing standards	Standards against which are measured the appropriateness of auditing procedures in relation to the objectives to be attained, the quality and extent of their application and the suitability of the resulting auditor's report.
auditing techniques	The methods of obtaining audit evidence, e.g. confirmation, observation and analysis. (Compare **auditing procedures**.)
auditor	A person who conducts an audit, either in an independent capacity or as an employee (internal auditor).
auditor's certificate	(*obs.*) Syn. for **auditor's report**.
auditor's opinion	See **auditor's report**. The opinion may be:
adverse opinion	An opinion that one or more of the financial statements, or the financial statements taken as a whole, do not provide fair presentation.
denial of opinion	The statement by an auditor that, for reasons which arose from his audit, he is unable to express an opinion as to whether the

financial statements provide fair presentation. (Compare **disclaimer.**)

piecemeal opinion

An opinion where the auditor, while giving an adverse opinion or a denial of opinion with respect to the financial statements taken as a whole, expresses an unqualified opinion on certain specific items in the financial statements.

qualified opinion

An opinion that includes a qualification with respect to one or several specific items in the financial statements.

unqualified opinion

An opinion given without reservation or qualification.

auditor's report

1. The formal document in which an auditor expresses his opinion as to whether financial statements of the organization present fairly its position as at a given date and the results of its operations for the period ended on that date in accordance with generally accepted accounting principles. 2. Any report by an auditor in accordance with the terms of his appointment.

authorized capital

See **share capital.**

average cost

See **cost allocation methods.**

average return on investment

An approximation of the rate of return on an investment by computing the ratio of the average annual earnings from the investment to the average investment.

average yield

1. The average return from a number of investments. 2. The average return from an investment over a period of time. See **yield to maturity.**

averaging

A concept under income tax legislation which mitigates the tax impact of large increases in income received by a taxpayer in a particular year. **General averaging** permits a taxpayer, where income in a taxation year exceeds a defined threshold amount, to calculate the tax or the excess over this amount in a special manner. **Forward averaging** permits a taxpayer to spread certain types of income over a number of future years through the purchase of a special income-averaging annuity contract.

B

back order

The part of an original order for goods or services from a customer that remains to be filled after a portion of the original order has been completed. (Compare **backlog.**)

backlog

Unfilled orders. (Compare **back order.**)

bad debt

An account or note receivable that is considered uncollectible. (Compare **doubtful account** or **doubtful debt.**)

bad debts recovered Collections on accounts previously written off as bad debts.

balance *n.* The excess of debits over credits or credits over debits in an account.

v.i. (of books and accounts). Books are said to balance when the totals of the debit and credit balances kept by double entry are equal or when the total of the balances of the accounts in a subsidiary ledger is in agreement with the balance of the controlling account.

v.t. 1. To determine that the totals of the debit and credit balances in books of account kept by double entry are equal. 2. To determine that the total of the balances of the accounts in a subsidiary ledger is in agreement with the balance of the controlling account.

balance sheet A formal statement of financial position, in the form of a concise statement, showing assets, liabilities, and owners' equity in a classified manner and as at a particular moment of time. The balance sheet is a statement of current resources, unexpired costs, liabilities to be met and sources of ownership funds, rather than a statement of economic worth.

balance sheet, form of The arrangement of the items in the balance sheet.

account form The total of the assets appears as an amount equal to the total of the liabilities and owners' equity. The assets are usually set on one side with the liabilities and owners' equity on the other.

double account form The balance sheet is shown in two sections, (1) the Capital Account containing those accounts relative to the cost of fixed assets, long-term liabilities, permanently invested capital, and the balancing amount which is carried to the General Account, and (2) the General Account containing current assets and liabilities, retained earnings, and the balancing amount carried from the Capital Account and any remaining items. This form is now rarely used except in fund accounting by municipalities and other public bodies.

financial position form The current liabilities are deducted from the current assets and then other liabilities are deducted from other assets to show net assets equivalent to the owners' equity.

report form The liabilities are deducted from the assets to show the owners' equity as the balance.

balance sheet audit See **audit.**

balance sheet equation The formula expressing the fundamental balance sheet relationships, namely, Assets = Liabilities + Owners' equity (or a variation of this formula, e.g. $A - L = 0$). The balance sheet equation is used to explain the equality of debits and credits in double entry bookkeeping.

bank confirmation A statement obtained by an auditor from his client's banker reporting the position, at a stated date, of the client's bank accounts, loans and other liabilities, security held against liabilities, and other matters.

bank discount	The amount deducted by a bank from the face amount or maturity value of a note, representing interest paid in advance.
bank reconciliation	See **reconciliation.**
bank statement	A list sent by a bank periodically (usually monthly) to its customers setting out all of the changes during the period in the customer's current or personal chequing account with the bank. The cheques charged against the account during the period are usually returned to the customer with the bank statement together with vouchers for other entries, if any, initiated by the bank.
bankrupt	The legal status of a person who has made an assignment in bankruptcy or against whom a receiving order has been made. See **assignment.**
bankruptcy	*n.* The state of being bankrupt. (Compare **insolvency.**)
barter transaction	An exchange of goods or services for other goods or services rather than for cash.
base stock method	See **cost allocation methods.**
basic earnings per share	See **earnings per share.**
basket purchase	Syn. for **lump-sum purchase.**
bearer security	A security not registered in the name of any owner or on which the last endorsement is in blank (the latter security is commonly said to be "street" form). Physical possession of the security may establish ownership.
beneficial owner	The real owner of an asset, usually a security, title to which is registered in the name of a trustee.
benefit	In a technical sense, a payment made to a recipient under the provisions of an insurance, pension or employment contract.
benefit based pension plan	See **pension plan.**
best efforts offering	An arrangement between an issuer of securities and an investment dealer whereby the dealer, instead of acting as underwriter, agrees to act as the issuer's agent and to do his best to sell securities receiving a commission for those sold.
betterment	(*obs.*) Syn. for **improvement.**
bid/asked price	The bid price is the price a prospective buyer offers for a security or commodity and the asked price is the price at which the owner of a security or commodity offers to sell. When these prices are quoted they are the highest bid to buy and the lowest offer to sell a security or commodity in a given market at a given time.
bill	*n.* Syn. for **invoice.** *v.* To render an account, i.e. to send an invoice or periodic statement.
bill of exchange	An unconditional order in writing, addressed by one person to another, signed by the person giving it, requiring the person to

	whom it is addressed to pay, on demand or at a fixed or determinable future time, a sum certain in money to or to the order of a specified person, or to bearer.
bill of lading	A memorandum given by carriers acknowledging the receipt of goods and which serves as a document of title to the goods consigned.
bill of materials	A specification of the nature and quantity of the materials and parts entering into a particular product.
bill payable	A draft or promissory note payable. See also **note payable.**
bill receivable	A draft or promissory note receivable. See also **note receivable.**
binary system	A number system using the base two compared, for example, to the decimal number system which uses the base ten. The binary system is often used in mechanical and electronic data processing systems.
blanket coverage	Protection under a contract of insurance afforded a class of property or persons which may fluctuate in quantity, quality or location.
block purchase **block trade**	A purchase or sale of a large number of securities as a unit. The securities involved may be either of the same or different types.
blocked currency	Currency which by law cannot be withdrawn from the issuing country or exchanged for the currency of another country.
blotter	A simple record, e.g. a day book, sometimes made as the transactions occur, to provide the information required for subsequent formal entries.
board of directors	The committee of persons elected by the members of an organization to be responsible for supervising its affairs (e.g. elected by the shareholders of a corporation).
body corporate	Syn. for **corporation.**
bond	1. A certificate of indebtedness, issued by a government or corporation, generally being one of a number of such certificates. The term usually implies the assets have been pledged as security. (Compare **debenture.**)
callable bond	A bond which may be redeemed by the issuer prior to maturity under conditions specified in the bond indenture.
collateral trust bond	A bond secured by deposit of other securities with a trustee.
coupon bond	A bond containing detachable interest coupons which are presented to the issuer for payment on specified due dates.
extendible bond	A bond which, at the option of the holder, may be extended beyond the stated maturity date or exchanged for a bond of the same issuer maturing at a later date.

income bond	A bond on which the payment of interest is contingent upon earnings.
mortgage bond	A bond secured by a mortgage.
retractable bond	A bond which, at the option of the holder, may be redeemed before its maturity date.
serial bonds	An issue of bonds which is redeemable in periodical instalments.
sinking fund bonds	Bonds issued under an indenture which requires that funds be regularly set aside from earnings to provide for full or partial repayment of the issue.
bond	2. An obligation in writing, sometimes supported by collateral, given by an individual or company to another individual or company to pay damages, or to indemnify against losses caused by a third party through non-performance of a contract or other duties or by defalcation, e.g. a builder's performance bond or an employee fidelity bond.
bond discount	See **discount** 2.
bond issue expenses	The costs incurred, when issuing bonds, including legal fees, costs of pledging security, advertising, selling and printing costs.
bond premium	See **premium** 1.
book debt	Syn. for **account payable** or **account receivable.**
book inventory	The inventory of merchandise, raw materials, and supplies presumed to be on hand, as shown by the accounting records.
book of account	Any book or record in which the operations and transactions of an organization are recorded in terms of money or some other unit of measurement and which constitutes part of the accounting system. The books of account include books of original entry and ledgers.
book of original entry	A book of account in which operations and transactions are recorded for the first time preparatory to summarization and/or posting to ledger accounts. See **journal.**
book profit	(*colloq.*) 1. Profit as shown by accounting records. 2. Unrealized profit.
book value	1. The amount at which an item appears in the books of account and financial statements. It should not be confused with the basis on which the amount is determined, e.g. cost, replacement cost, liquidation value. The term is not an appropriate description of a basis of valuation of assets. 2. In connection with owners' equity in a business, the amount of the net assets of the business shown in a balance sheet.
bookkeeping	The process of classifying and recording business transactions in terms of money or some other unit of measurement in the books of account. (Compare **accounting** 1.)

break-even chart	Any of several types of charts on which the break-even point is shown; a projection of operations for a period in which costs and profits are shown for varying sales volumes.
break-even point	The level of operations of a business at which revenues equal expenses. It is usually expressed as the dollar volume of sales required to cover both fixed and variable expenses. If the amount of fixed expenses and the percentage of variable expenses to sales are known, the sales required to break even may be computed by solving the equation $S = F.E. + aS$, where S = sales to break even, $F.E.$ = amount of fixed expenses, a = percentage of variable expenses to sales.
break-up value	Syn. for **liquidation value.**
broken period	(*colloq.*) Any period not coinciding with the regular reporting period.
broker	1. A middleman or limited agent, often acting for both parties to a transaction. (Compare **agent.**) 2. (*colloq.*) A stockbroker.
brokerage fees	The fees or commission charged by a broker as remuneration for his services.
budget	A detailed estimate of future transactions, either in terms of quantities, or money values or both, designed to provide a plan for and control over future operations and activities. (Compare **forecast; projection.**)
capital budget	A budget for proposed additions to capital assets and their financing.
continuous budget	A budget which is updated systematically by adding the next week, month or quarter as a period of similar length just ended is dropped.
fixed budget	A budget which is prepared for a single level of activity.
flexible budget	A budget which is prepared for a range of levels of activity.
variable budget	Syn. for **flexible budget.**
budget variance	Syn. for **variance** 2.
budgetary control	The process of planning, executing, and evaluating a program of business activities by the use of a budget.
burden	Syn. for **overhead—factory overhead** or **factory service.**
business combination	Any transaction whereby one economic unit unites with or obtains control over another economic unit regardless of the legal avenue by which such control is obtained and regardless of the resultant form of the economic unit emerging from the transaction. A **conglomerate** business combination involves economic units operating in widely different industries. A **horizontal** business combination involves economic units whose products are similar. A **vertical** business combination involves economic units where the output from one can be used as input for the other.

acquisition Any transaction whereby one economic unit obtains control over another economic unit.

amalgamation The fusion of two or more corporations by transfer of their assets and liabilities to a new corporation. (Compare **merger.**)

merger The fusion of two or more corporations by transfer of the assets and liabilities to one of the constituent companies. (Compare **amalgamation.**)

statutory amalgamation A business combination in which two or more corporations incorporated under the same statute are combined and continue as one corporate entity. (Compare **amalgamation.**)

business combination, method of accounting for

new entity method A method of accounting for a business combination which views the resulting entity as a new entity and records net assets at fair values on the date of the combination. (Compare **pooling of interests method; purchase method.**)

pooling of interests method A method of accounting for a business combination under which the net assets are carried in the combined corporation's financial statements at their book values in the combining corporation's books. Income of the combined corporation comprises income of the combining corporations for the entire fiscal period in which the combination took place. (Compare **new entity method; purchase method.**)

purchase method A method of accounting for a business combination under which the net assets acquired are carried in the acquiring corporation's financial statements at their cost to the acquiring corporation. Income of the acquiring corporation includes income of the acquired corporation from the date of acquisition. (Compare **new entity method; pooling of interests method.**)

business interruption insurance See **insurance.**

buy and sell insurance agreement

buy-out insurance Cross insurance by partners for the purpose of providing funds to purchase the deceased's share in the partnership on the death of a partner.

buyers' market A condition within an industry or geographic area where the supply of a product or service exceeds the demand; hence trading conditions favour the buyer. (Compare **sellers' market.**)

by-law 1. A secondary or subordinate law dealing with matters of local or internal regulation. 2. In an organization, the rules formally approved by the owners or members to regulate the method of operation.

by-product A marketable product of lesser importance produced incidentally with a major product. (Compare **joint products.**)

C

C. & F.
(*abbr.*) Cost and freight. A condition of sale where the price includes charges for handling and freight up to delivery to a specified location. (Compare **C.I.F.; F.A.S.** and **F.O.B.**)

call
With reference to share capital, a payment requested by the directors on a subscription, or an amount otherwise due under the terms of a subscription agreement.

call loan
Syn. for **demand loan.**

callable bond
See **bond** 1.

cancelled cheque
See **cheque.**

cancelled share
See **share.**

Cansaf report
The long form report prepared by finance companies containing detailed information concerning receivables, debt outstanding, etc., as recommended by the Canadian Association of Sales Finance Companies.

capacity
The maximum ability of a resource or organizational unit to provide goods or services.

   ideal or theoretical capacity
The maximum level of production of which a resource or organizational unit is capable, making no allowance for normal interruptions such as work stoppages or repairs.

   idle capacity
The portion of capacity that is not used due to lack of product demand, errors in planning or similar causes.

   normal capacity
The maximum level of production of a resource or organizational unit under normal circumstances.

capital
1. The interest of the owner or proprietors in the assets of a business. Capital in this sense is often called owners' equity, proprietorship equity, net assets or net worth, and is represented by the excess of the total assets over the total liabilities to outside interests. 2. In a limited company, that portion of the equity contributed by the shareholders which may be returned to the shareholders only after compliance with the formalities imposed by the governing act or the instrument of incorporation. 3. The total funds provided by lenders (usually restricted to long-term lenders) and by owners for the use of the business.

capital account
1. An account for part or all of the owners' equity. Often limited to that portion of the owners' equity that is deemed to be permanent. 2. See **balance sheet, form of—double account form**

capital asset
1. An asset, whether tangible or intangible, intended for long-term use and held as such. (Compare **fixed asset.**)
2. (*government accounting*) Any asset of the capital fund. See **balance sheet, form of—double account form.**

capital budget
See **budget.**

capital cost allowance	A deduction, akin to depreciation, allowed in computing income for income tax purposes.
capital expenditure	An expenditure to acquire or add to a capital asset; an expenditure yielding enduring benefits.
capital fund	See **fund accounting.**
capital gain	1. Profit on the sale or disposition of a capital asset. 2. A gain resulting from a scaling down of business debts as in a reorganization, an arrangement with creditors, or a purchase of the company's own bonds at a discount. 3. Under income tax legislation, the term has a special meaning.
capital impairment	The amount by which the permanent equity contribution from the owners exceeds the net assets of an organization.
capital leverage	See **leverage.**
capital loss	1. Loss on sale or disposition of a capital asset. 2. Under income tax legislation, the term has a special meaning.
capital stock	The ownership interest in a limited company authorized by its instrument of incorporation. See also **share capital.**
common stock	The class of capital stock representing the residual equity in the company's assets and earnings.
cumulative stock	A class of preferred capital stock entitled to payment of cumulative dividends.
non-cumulative stock	A class of preferred capital stock in which the right to a dividend lapses annually.
ordinary stock	Syn. for **common stock.**
participating stock	A class of preferred capital stock which, in addition to a dividend at a fixed annual rate, participates with common stock in the distribution of profits and sometimes in the residual distribution on liquidation of the company.
preferred stock	A class of capital stock with special rights or restrictions as compared with other classes of stock of the same company. The preference will generally attach to the distribution of dividends at a fixed annual rate, with or without priority for return of capital on liquidation. The restrictions generally apply to voting rights.
redeemable stock	A class of capital stock callable for redemption at the option of the company in accordance with conditions determined by the instrument of incorporation.
capital structure	The classification by nature of the claims of lenders (usually restricted to long-term lenders) and owners against the business.
capital surplus	See **surplus.**
capitalization	1. Syn. for **capital structure.** 2. The computation of the present value of future income. 3. See **capitalize.**
capitalize	1. To charge an expenditure to a capital asset account rather

than to an expense account. 2. To appropriate retained earnings for permanent retention, e.g. by the issue of a stock dividend. 3. To provide capital for a purpose.

carry back See **carry-over.**

carry forward See **carry-over.**

carry-over Under income tax legislation, the right to apply a current loss against the taxable income of allowable prior periods (carry back) and/or against the taxable income of allowable future periods (carry forward).

carrying charge 1. A cost associated with the ownership, as distinct from the acquisition, of property. 2. An addition to the selling price of an article sold on the instalment plan, e.g. interest and/or administration charge.

carrying value Syn. for **book value.**

cash 1. Legal tender. 2. Coin, bank notes, money orders, postal notes, cheques and accepted sight drafts, and (by extension) the balances in respect of demand and savings deposits at banks or other financial institutions.

cash audit See **audit.**

cash basis of accounting The method of recording transactions by which revenues and expenditures are reflected in the accounts in the period in which the related cash receipts or disbursements occur. (Compare **accrual basis of accounting.**)

cash book A book of original entry for recording cash received and paid out. In practice, the cash book is frequently replaced by two separate books, one to record receipts of cash, the other payments.

cash discount See **discount** *n.*1.

cash flow The figure resulting from adding back to income items that do not affect working capital, such as depreciation and amortization. Used chiefly by financial analysts and not to be confused with ''cash flow'' as used in the **cash flow statement.**

cash flow per share The cash flow for a particular period of time divided by the number of common shares outstanding.

cash flow statement See **statement, cash flow.**

cash statement Syn. for **statement of receipts and disbursements.**

cash surrender value The amount recoverable on cancellation of some types of life insurance policies. This is often the limit of the amount which the insured can borrow against the policy.

certified cheque See **cheque.**

changes in financial position, statement of See **statement of changes in financial position.**

changes in net assets, statement of See **statement of changes in net assets.**

charge	*n.* Syn. for **debit** *n.*
	v. Syn. for **debit** *v.*
charge account	The arrangement between a supplier and a customer which allows the customer to obtain goods or services on stipulated credit terms.
charge and discharge, statement of	See **statement of charge and discharge**.
charge off	*v.* To treat as an expense or a loss an item originally recorded as an asset; to write off.
chart of accounts	A list of the account numbers and designations in a ledger.
charter	*n.* The letters patent, special Act or other instrument of incorporation.
chattel mortgage	See **mortgage**.
check	*n.* 1. Control or supervision to secure accuracy. 2. (*U.S.*) Cheque.
	v.t. 1. To verify accuracy. 2. To place a mark on an item after verifying it.
check list	A pre-listed series of instructions or questions to be followed in the review of a given set of methods and practices.
cheque	A bill of exchange drawn on a bank, payable on demand.
cancelled cheque	A cheque that has been honoured by the bank on which it was drawn, and bears on its face evidence of payment.
certified cheque	A cheque payment of which is guaranteed by the bank on which it is drawn.
stale-dated cheque	A cheque which has not been presented to the bank on which it is drawn for payment within a reasonable time of its date (generally six months in Canada by the custom of bankers) and which may therefore be dishonoured by the bank without any breach of the banker-customer contract.
cheque register	A book of original entry in which cheques issued are recorded.
C.I.F.	(*abbr.*) Cost, insurance and freight. A condition of sale where the price includes charges for handling, insurance and freight up to delivery to a specified location. (Compare **C. & F.**; **F.A.S.** and **F.O.B.**)
circularization	The act or result of circularizing. See **confirmation**.
circularize	To communicate with a group to get their reaction to the contents of the communication; to confirm by correspondence.
circulating capital	Syn. for **working capital**.
classification	The allocation or grouping of items in accounts or statements according to a pattern. Expenditures, for example, may be classified by character, e.g. in governmental accounting as current expenses, provision for debt retirement, or capital outlay; by function, e.g. production, distribution, finance, etc.;

by activity, e.g. mixing, grinding, shipping, etc.; or by object, e.g. a specific article or service.

clean report   (*colloq.*) An unqualified opinion. See **auditor's opinion.**

clean surplus (form)   Syn. for **all-inclusive income statement** (form).

clearing account   An account used as a temporary repository for amounts of a recurring nature which are eventually transferred to other accounts. (Compare **suspense account.**)

clearing house   An organization that facilitates transfer transactions among members of an industry, profession or other group; e.g. a bank clearing house allows daily settlements to be made among banks for cheques drawn, deposits transferred, etc.

close   *v.* To make closing entries in the books of account.

close corporation   Syn. for **closely-held corporation.**

closed-end   *adj.* Relating to the capital structure of an organization where shares or units of participation once issued are transferable but cannot be cancelled or redeemed except by resolution of the shareholders or unitholders or under regulation or legislation. (Compare **open-end.**)

closed-end fund
closed-end investment company   See **investment company.**

closely-held corporation   A corporation in which the shares are held by a small number of shareholders.

closing entry   An entry made at the end of an accounting period for the purpose of transferring the balances in nominal accounts to the income, retained earnings, capital, or owners' current accounts.

C.O.D.   (*abbr.*) Cash on delivery. A condition of sale where the purchaser is required to pay the purchase price in cash immediately upon delivery of goods.

co-insurance   See **insurance.**

collateral   *n.* (*colloq.*) Syn. for **security** 2.

collateral note   Syn. for **secured note.**

collateral security   Security which is given in addition to the principal security and only to be resorted to after the principal security has been realized upon.

collateral trust bond   See **bond** 1.

combined financial statement   A composite financial statement comprising the accounts of two or more companies which may or may not be related. (Compare **consolidated financial statements.**)

comfort letter   A letter by which an auditor conveys negative assurance as to unaudited financial statements in a prospectus or draft financial statements included in a preliminary prospectus.

commercial paper	Short-term unsecured promissory notes issued by financial institutions and industrial corporations.
common cost	A cost which is not directly traceable to specific segments of the organization.
common revenue	Revenue which is not directly applicable to specific segments of the organization.
common share	See **share**. See also **capital stock**.
common-size statement	See **statement, common-size**.
common stock	See **capital stock**.
common stock equivalent	(*U.S.*) A security which, because of its terms and the circumstances under which it was issued, is regarded as equivalent to a common share for purposes of calculating the earnings per share.
company	Any association, whether incorporated or unincorporated, of persons who are joined in a common interest, generally for the purpose of carrying on a business undertaking. (Compare **corporation; limited company**.)
comparative statement	A form of financial statement presentation in which current amounts and corresponding amounts from previous periods or dates are set out together.
completed contract method	A method of accounting which recognizes income only when the goods to be provided or the services to be rendered are completed or substantially so. (Compare **percentage-of-completion method**.)
composite life depreciation	See **depreciation unit**.
compound entry	A journal entry in which there is more than one debit or more than one credit.
comprehensive tax allocation	Syn. for **tax allocation—interperiod tax allocation**.
comptroller	A title given to an officer or senior employee of an organization whose responsibilities generally involve the accounting control functions of the organization.
condensed financial statements	Financial statements in which less important detail is combined for the purpose of providing a readily comprehensible picture of financial position.
conditional discharge	The release of a bankrupt debtor from his contractual liabilities subject to the fulfilment of certain specified conditions.
conditional sales agreement	A contract of sale in which the transfer of title is deferred until specified payments have been made.
confirmation	(*auditing*) Verification from sources other than the books and records under review. Usually this is accomplished by correspondence with a third party, such as a customer, creditor or bank. The confirmation is known as positive if the

third party is requested to reply in any event, and as negative if a reply is requested only in the case of disagreement.

conglomerate business combination

See **business combination.**

conglomerate company

Syn. for **diversified company.**

conservatism

An accounting postulate which stipulates that, in a situation where acceptable alternative accounting procedures may be used, the one that produces lower current amounts for income and assets ought to be chosen.

consignee

See **consignment.**

consignment

A shipment of goods made under an agreement whereby the receiver (the consignee) undertakes to sell or otherwise dispose of the goods as agent on behalf of the shipper (the consignor). The latter retains title to the goods until they are sold or disposed of according to the agreement.

consignor

See **consignment.**

consistency

An accounting postulate which stipulates that the same accounting procedures should be followed from period to period by an organization in the preparation and presentation of its financial statements.

consolidated financial statements

The financial statements of a parent company and one or more of its subsidiaries combined so as to ignore the separate legal identities of the companies and show the financial position and operating results of the group as one economic unit. (Compare **combined financial statement.**)

consolidated goodwill

The excess of cost of the shares to an acquiring corporation over the amounts assigned to its equity in the fair value of the identifiable net assets of the acquired corporation at the date of acquisition. (Compare **purchase discrepancy.**)

consolidation (of shares)

Reduction in the number of shares of a class of capital stock, with no change in the total dollar amount of the class, but with a converse increase in the par or stated value of the shares. This is achieved by replacing one new share for a specified number of old shares. (Compare **stock split.**)

constant dollars

Dollars of a given base year into which dollars of the year under study are restated for the purpose of eliminating the effect of fluctuations in purchasing power.

constrained share company

A public company whose instrument of incorporation specifies that at least a certain prescribed percentage of the shares must be beneficially owned by persons who are Canadian citizens or who are corporations resident in Canada.

consumed cost

Any cost the benefits from which have expired or have been lost or destroyed; any cost that has been recognized as an item to be charged in the income statement.

consumer price index

See **price index.**

contingency fund	Cash or investments set aside or reserved for unforeseen expenditures.
contingency reserve	See **reserve.**
contingent asset	Something of potential value depending on the occurrence or non-occurrence of some specific future event, e.g. a general insurance policy represents a contingent asset to the insured.
contingent issuance	In the calculation of earnings per share, a possible issue of common shares that is dependent upon the conversion of senior shares or debt, the exercise of rights, warrants or options, the satisfaction of certain conditions or similar arrangements.
contingent liability	A legal obligation that may arise in the future out of past and/or present circumstances provided certain developments occur.
contingent merger contract	A business combination contract under which the acquirer pays a lump sum at the time of the transaction with provision for additional payment to the vendor if certain conditions are met, e.g. specified earnings levels attained or maintained for a specified period.
continuity concept	Syn. for **going concern concept.**
continuous audit	See **audit.**
continuous budget	See **budget.**
contra account	An account that wholly or partially offsets another account, e.g. mutual claims against each other by two parties.
contract	*n.* An agreement, intended to give rise to legal obligations, entered into between two or more persons to do or abstain from doing something.
contributed capital	See **share capital.**
contributed surplus	See **surplus.**
contributed surplus, statement of	See **statement of contributed surplus.**
contribution margin	1. The excess of sales price over related variable expenses. 2. Syn. for **segment margin.**
contributory pension plan	See **pension plan.**
control	*n.* 1. The power to influence actions (e.g. a controlling interest in a limited company is possessed by anyone, or any group, being able to elect the majority of the company's directors). 2. See **accounting control.**
controlled company	1. A corporation which is under the control of another corporation or person. 2. Under income tax and corporations legislation, the term has a special meaning.
controller	Syn. for **comptroller.**
control(ling) account	A general ledger account, the balance of which represents the total of the balances of the accounts in a subsidiary ledger.
controlling interest	See **control 1.**

26

controlling shareholder	A shareholder who has the power to elect at least a majority of the board of directors.
conversion cost	The cost of changing an existing resource from one form or function to another, e.g. the cost of direct labour and facility overhead incurred in transforming raw materials into finished products.
conversion of foreign currency	The act of exchanging the currency of one country for the currency of another country. (Compare **translation of foreign currency**.)
convertible	1. A feature attached to some securities permitting the owners to exchange the securities for the securities of another class in accordance with specified conditions. 2. Of currency, capable of being exchanged for the currency of another country.
co-operative	*n.* An incorporated organization formed for the benefit of its members (owners) who are either producers or consumers in order to acquire for them profits or savings which would otherwise accrue to middlemen. Control is exercised by the members on the basis of one vote per member.
copyright	*n.* The exclusive right, conferred by *The Copyright Act* (Canada), to produce or reproduce an original literary, dramatic, musical or artistic work. In general, the term of copyright protection is for the life of the author and fifty years after his death.
corporate joint venture	A joint venture entered into by the parties through the vehicle of a corporation.
corporation	A legal entity, with or without share capital, separate and distinct from its owners or persons who constituted it, which has all the rights and responsibilities of a person except those rights which only a natural person can exercise. (Compare **company; limited company.**)
corpus	The principal or capital of an estate, as opposed to its income.
correcting entry	An entry made for the purpose of rectifying an error in the books of account. (Compare **correction of error.**)
correction of error	The process of adjustment arising from occasions when errors relating to previously issued financial statements are discovered. (Compare **correcting entry; prior period adjustment.**)
correlation analysis	See **analysis**.
cost	The amount, measured in money, of the expenditure to obtain goods or services. See **expired cost; unexpired cost.** (Compare **expense; loss.**)
cost accounting	That branch of accounting concerned with the classification, recording, analysis, reporting and interpretation of expenditures identifiable with the production and distribution of goods and services.

cost accounting method	Any method of product costing.
absorption costing	A costing method in which fixed manufacturing expenses are included in inventory valuation in addition to direct materials, direct labour and variable overhead charges.
direct costing	A costing method in which only direct materials, direct labour and variable overhead are charged to inventory. All fixed manufacturing expenses are regarded as period costs and therefore excluded from inventory valuation.
estimated cost system	A costing method in which the recorded costs of production are initially based on estimated costs with later adjustments for any differences between estimated and actual.
job cost system **job order costing**	A costing method in which costs for each distinguishable unit or batch are determined by accumulating the costs that are identifiable with it during the entire production process. (Compare **process cost system; process costing.**)
prime costing	(*Br.*) A costing method in which both fixed and variable overhead are regarded as period costs and therefore excluded from inventory valuation.
process cost system **process costing**	A costing method in which costs for non-distinguishable units of production are determined by accumulating the costs of the production process over a period of time and dividing by the number of units produced. (Compare **job cost system; job order costing.**)
standard cost system **standard costing**	A costing method in which costs of production are recorded on the basis of predetermined standards with a view to achieving control through analysis of variances between actual and standard conditions. See **variance** 2.
cost allocation methods	There are several methods of allocating costs between inventory and cost of sales. In most cases, the cost of items sold or consumed during a period is arrived at by deducting the costs attributable to items on hand at the end of the period from the total costs accumulated during the period.
average cost	The cost of an item is determined by applying a weighted average of the cost of all similar items at a point of time or over a period.
base stock method	The cost of items sold or consumed during a period is determined by assuming that a predetermined minimum quantity of materials or merchandise is carried in inventory permanently and at a fixed price.
FIFO	(*abbr.*) First in, first out. The cost of items sold or consumed during a period is computed as though the items were sold or consumed in order of their acquisition.
LIFO	(*abbr.*) Last in, first out. The cost of items sold or consumed during a period is deemed to be the cost of the most recent acquisitions.
NIFO	(*abbr.*) Next in, first out. The cost of items sold or consumed during a period is deemed to be the cost of the next acquisition in the following period.

specific identification	The actual cost of each item is ascertained separately.
cost based pension plan	See **pension plan.**
cost/benefit analysis	See **analysis.**
cost centre	A unit, group or subdivision within an organization with which costs are identified for purposes of managerial control.
cost ledger	A subsidiary ledger containing accounts relating exclusively to cost accounting.
cost method	A basis of accounting for intercorporate investments whereby the investment is recorded at cost and the post-acquisition earnings of the investee are recognized only to the extent received as dividends. (Compare **equity method.**)
cost of capital	The cost, expressed as a yield rate, of investment funds whether obtained through borrowing, equity investment or retention of earnings.
cost of goods sold **cost of sales**	The total cost of goods sold during an accounting period. In a manufacturing operation, it includes the cost of materials, labour and overhead; selling and administrative expenses are normally excluded.
cost-plus contract	A contract under which the contractor is to recover the costs incurred in performing the contract plus an agreed markup or fee. (Compare **fixed price contract.**)
cost sheet	A summary of all of the cost elements of a particular product or service.
cost/volume/profit analysis	See **analysis.**
coupon bond	See **bond** 1.
coupon rate	The rate of interest that is to be paid on a coupon bond as specified in the indenture.
credit	*n.* 1. The ability to buy or borrow in consideration of a promise to pay at a later date. 2. An entry recording the creation of or addition to a liability, or owners' equity, or revenue, or the reduction or elimination of an asset or expense. (Converse of **debit**.) *v.* To record a credit entry in books of account.
credit memorandum **credit note**	A document prepared by the seller notifying the purchaser that his account is being reduced by a stated amount because of an allowance, return or cancellation. (Compare **debit memorandum; invoice**.)
credit report	A report issued by a credit bureau giving factual information about an individual or corporation which may bear on a decision to grant credit to that individual or corporation.
credit union	A savings and loan institution organized on a co-operative basis to provide savings and loan services to and for the benefit of its members (owners).

creditor	One to whom a debt is owed.
ordinary creditor	1. A person who, by statute, is entitled to satisfaction of his proven claim against the estate of a bankrupt only after the claims of all other classes of creditors have been satisfied. 2. *(colloq.)* An unsecured creditor.
preferred creditor	A person who, by statute, is entitled to full satisfaction of his proven claim against the estate of a bankrupt before other unsecured creditors receive anything.
secured creditor	A person whose claim against a debtor is supported by certain assets which have been pledged to the creditor or upon which the creditor has a lien.
cremation certificate	A sworn statement by a trustee or other agent that certain documents listed in the statement have been destroyed.
Critical Path Method	A method of network analysis in which normal duration time is estimated for each activity within a project. The critical path identifies the shortest completion period based on the most time-consuming sequence of activities from the beginning to the end of the network. (Compare **PERT**.)
crossfoot	*v.* To add horizontally the totals of vertical columns of figures.
Crown corporation	A corporation that is ultimately accountable through a Minister of the Crown to Parliament or a legislature for the conduct of its affairs.
cum div. or **cum dividend**	The condition of shares whose quoted market price includes a declared but unpaid dividend. This condition pertains between the declaration date of the dividend and the record date. (Compare **ex div.** or **ex dividend.**)
cum rights	The condition of securities whose quoted market price includes the right to purchase new securities. (Compare **ex rights.**)
cumulative dividends	See **dividend** 1.
cumulative share	See **share**. See also **capital stock.**
cumulative stock	See **capital stock.**
cumulative voting	A method of electing a board of directors whereby the owner of any one share is allowed as many votes as there are directors to be elected. The votes may be allocated by the shareholder to one or more candidates at his discretion.
current account	A running account with a person or organization. A bank current account is usually a chequing account as contrasted with a savings account; a partner's current account is a record of his drawings and his portion of profits available for withdrawal, as contrasted with his permanent investment in the business which is reflected in his capital account. (Compare **account current.**)
current asset	Unrestricted cash or other asset that, in the normal course of operations, is expected to be converted into cash or consumed in the production of income within one year or within the normal operating cycle where that is longer than a year. (Compare **liquid assets; quick assets.**)

current liability	A liability whose regular and ordinary liquidation is expected to occur within one year or within the normal operating cycle where that is longer than a year. A liability otherwise classified as current but for which provision has been made for payment from other than current resources should be excluded.
current maturities	The portion of long term obligations to be retired during the ensuing twelve months, normally classified as a current liability.
current operating performance concept	The view that unusual and non-recurring operating items which occurred during an accounting period should be excluded from the income statement. (Compare **all-inclusive income statement** (form).)
current ratio	See **ratio analysis.**
current service pension cost	See **pension costs.**
current value accounting	A general term designating methods of accounting based on current value rather than historical cost. The valuation bases include, for example, reproduction cost, replacement cost, resale price and present value.
cut-off	A notional break in the continuity of the recording of the flow of transactions or in the physical flow of goods, assumed as of a point of time.
cycle billing	A method of billing customers by specific groups throughout the accounting period so that all customers are billed once in each period. This method is in contrast to billing all customers as at one particular date.

D

data bank	An organized file of information, such as a customer name and address file, used in and kept up-to-date by the processing system.
data centre	A data processing installation that provides data processing services to different users. The term is generally restricted to mechanical or electronic installations.
data processing	A generic term for the operations carried out in assembling, classifying, recording, analyzing and reporting of information by manual, mechanical or electronic means.
dated retained earnings	Retained earnings of a corporation accumulated from the date of a reorganization or quasi-reorganization.
day book	A chronological record of transactions of an enterprise, particularly relating to merchandise. Day books have largely been supplanted by copies of invoices, cash register tapes, etc.
days of grace	The days allowed by law for payment of a debt after its due date.

31

debenture

A certificate of indebtedness issued by a government or company, generally being one of a number of such certificates. The term usually implies an unsecured obligation. (Compare **bond** 1.)

debit

n. An entry recording the creation of, or addition to, an asset, the incurring of an expense, or the reduction or elimination of a liability, owners' equity or revenue. (Converse of **credit** 2.)

v. To record a debit entry in books of account.

debit memorandum
debit note

A document prepared by the purchaser notifying the seller that his account has been reduced by a stated amount because of an allowance, return or cancellation. (Compare **credit memorandum; credit note; invoice.**)

debt

A sum of money owing by one person (the debtor) to another (the creditor) payable either on demand or at some fixed or determinable future time.

declaration

1. (of dividend) The formal act of a corporation which creates a liability for a dividend. 2. Any formal document attesting a fact, as, for example, the statement given by the insured to the insurer, upon which the risk in underwriting an insurance contract is based.

declaration date

The date on which the board of directors of a corporation declares a dividend.

deduction at source

A deduction made by a payer from amounts paid to the payee and remitted by the payer to a third party under the terms of a statute or private agreement.

defalcation

See **embezzlement.**

default

Failure to fulfill the terms of a contract or agreement, e.g. failure to pay debt interest or principal when due.

deferment
deferral

An item of revenue received or receivable or expense incurred, applicable to a subsequent period, and accordingly carried forward on the balance sheet for disposition in a future period. See **deferred charge; deferred credit; deferred revenue.**

deferral method

See **tax allocation—interperiod tax allocation.**

deferred charge

1. A long-term expense prepayment; an expenditure, other than a capital expenditure, the benefit of which will extend over a period of years from the time of incurrence and meanwhile is carried forward to be charged to expense over a period of years. (Compare **prepaid expense** 1.) 2. Balance of amounts paid for goods or services received for which the payee has no further obligation and meanwhile is carried forward to be charged to expense in future years. (Compare **prepaid expense** 2.)

deferred compensation plan

A plan by which payment for services rendered by employees is deferred until some specified future time.

deferred credit	1. An amount received, recorded as receivable or (as in deferred income taxes) provided for, that represents a reduction of future expenses. 2. Syn. for **deferred income** or **deferred revenue.**
deferred income	An amount of income received or recorded as receivable but not yet earned.
deferred income taxes	The accumulated amounts by which income taxes charged in the accounts have been increased (accumulated tax allocation credit) or decreased (accumulated tax allocation debit) as a result of timing differences.
deferred profit-sharing plan	See **profit-sharing plan.**
deferred revenue	An amount of revenue received or recorded as receivable but not yet earned.
deferred tax credit	See **deferred income taxes.**
deferred tax debit	See **deferred income taxes.**
deficiency account	1. A statement of an insolvent debtor which accounts for the excess of liabilities over the estimated realizable value of the assets. 2. The ledger account showing the deficiency of assets upon realization and liquidation.
deficit	See **surplus—retained earnings.**
defined contribution pension plan	Syn. for **pension plan—cost based.**
demand deposit	A deposit in a bank or other financial institution that may be withdrawn on demand. (Compare **time deposit.**)
demand loan	A loan repayable at the will of the lender and to which days of grace are not applicable. (Compare **term loan.**)
demurrage	A charge made by the carrier for a delay in loading or unloading a vessel (including a ship, railway car or other vehicle) beyond the time specified.
denial of opinion	See **auditor's opinion.**
depletion	1. A reduction in quantity of wasting assets, as a result of consumption or removal of natural resources, e.g. standing timber, mineral deposits. 2. A charge in an accounting period to reflect the cost of the portion of wasting assets consumed or removed in that period.
deposit	1. A lodgement of cash, securities, etc. with others. 2. A payment to a bank or other financial institution by or for a customer for credit to his account. 3. Syn. for **downpayment.**
deposit certificate	A certificate showing that a deposit of a specified amount has been made at a bank or trust company for a specified period of time, usually less than five years, and at a specified rate of interest. The certificate may be redeemable before maturity at the option of the holder, subject to an interest penalty. (Compare **guaranteed investment certificate.**)

depreciated cost	Cost less accumulated depreciation.
depreciated value	Syn. for **amortized value**.
depreciation	1. The gradual exhaustion of the service capacity of fixed assets which is not restored by maintenance practices. It is the consequence of such factors as use, obsolescence, inadequacy, and decay. 2. The expense in an accounting period arising from the application of depreciation accounting.
depreciation accounting	An accounting procedure in which the cost or other recorded value of a fixed asset less estimated residual value (if any) is distributed over its estimated useful life in a systematic and rational manner. It is a process of allocation, not valuation. (Compare **renewal accounting; retirement accounting**.)
depreciation base	The cost or other recorded value of a fixed asset less estimated residual value, if any, to be charged to expense through the process of depreciation accounting.
depreciation method	Any method of calculating depreciation for an accounting period.
annuity method	The method in which the periodic charge is computed as a constant amount equal to the sum of (1) a constant amount; (2) interest at a specified rate compounded annually on the accumulated amount, which together with item (1) will equal the depreciation base by the estimated date of retirement; and (3) interest on the declining investment in the asset. The amount credited annually to accumulated depreciation is the sum of items (1) and (2); item (3) is credited to income so that the effect on net income is limited to items (1) and (2).
diminishing balance method	The method in which the periodic charge is computed as a constant fraction of the depreciated cost so that the depreciation base is written off by the estimated date of retirement.
production method	The method in which the periodic charge is that proportion of the depreciation base that the production or use during the period bears to the total estimated production or use to be obtained from the asset.
reducing balance method	Syn. for **diminishing balance method**.
service-output method	Syn. for **production method**.
sinking fund method	The method in which the periodic charge is computed as the sum of (1) a constant amount and (2) interest at a specified rate compounded annually on the accumulated amount, so that the total of the periodic provisions will equal the depreciation base by the estimated date of retirement.
straight-line method	The method in which the periodic charge is computed by dividing the depreciation base by the estimated number of periods of service life.
sum-of-the-years'-digits method	The method in which the depreciation base is allocated to the

individual years on a reducing basis by multiplying it by a fraction in which the numerator is the number of years + 1 of estimated life remaining, and the denominator is the sum of the series of numbers representing the years in the total estimated life. For an asset having an estimated life of five years, the denominator is 15 (i.e. 1 + 2 + 3 + 4 + 5), and the numerator for the first year is 5, for the second year 4, and so on.

depreciation rate

A percentage which when applied to the depreciation base (or, in the case of the diminishing balance method, the depreciation base less accumulated depreciation) will produce the depreciation expense for the period.

depreciation unit

The individual asset (unit or item depreciation) or group of similar assets (group or composite life depreciation) which are treated as a unit for the purposes of depreciation accounting.

designated surplus

A term in income tax legislation; broadly, the retained earnings on hand in a corporation at the time when control is acquired by another corporation.

detailed audit

See **audit.**

development costs
development expense

1. Expenditures made to bring a mineral property or other natural resources into production. 2. Expenditures made in promoting a new product or enterprise.

differential cost

Syn. for **marginal cost.**

diminishing balance method

See **depreciation method.**

direct cost

An item of cost that can be reasonably identified with a specific unit of product or with a specific operation or other cost centre.

direct costing

See **cost accounting method.**

direct labour

The cost of labour applied to the material that will form an integral part of the final product in a manufacturing process.

direct material

See **material.**

direct overhead

See **overhead.**

director

See **board of directors.**

disbursement

An outlay of cash. (Compare **expenditure.**)

discharge

The legal effect of the repayment of a debt or the performance of an obligation or the release of a person from an obligation (e.g. the release of a bankrupt from claims provable in bankruptcy upon completion of the processes of bankruptcy).

disclaimer

A written communication, usually entitled "Accountant's Comments" or "Disclaimer of Opinion", accompanying financial statements prepared by, or with the assistance of, a public accountant setting out that, since the terms of the engagement did not call for an expression of opinion on the financial statements, he has not performed an audit and consequently no opinion is being expressed. (Compare **auditor's opinion—denial of opinion.**)

disclosure

That aspect of financial reporting that is concerned with the proper amount of detailed information to be provided in the financial statements.

discount

n. 1. A reduction from a list price or a stated amount.

cash discount

A reduction of debt granted by a creditor in consideration of payment within a prescribed time.

quantity discount

A reduction in the selling price of goods or services granted by a vendor in consideration of the large number of units purchased in an individual transaction. (Compare **volume discount.**)

trade discount

A deduction from the list price of goods applying to customers or purchasers of a particular class or type, usually merchants purchasing for resale.

volume discount

A reduction in the selling price of goods or services granted by a vendor in consideration of the large number of units purchased over a stated period. (Compare **quantity discount.**)

discount

n. 2. The amount by which the selling price of a security is less than its par value. (Compare **premium** 1.) 3. The amount deducted, as interest in advance, from the maturity value of a note when it is sold to a bank for its present worth, usually with a guarantee; or any similar difference between present worth and value at maturity.

v. 1. To sell for its present worth, either with or without recourse, a note or other claim or right to future value. 2. To compute the present value of a future sum.

discounted cash flow

A method of evaluating return on a proposed investment which takes into consideration the time value of money.

discounted value

The value at a given date of a future payment determined by applying compound interest at a given rate to the payment.

discovered asset

An asset that is recognized as the result of discovery, e.g. minerals.

distributable surplus

See **surplus.**

distribution

1. Disposition, usually final, of the assets of a business or estate upon winding up. 2. Under securities legislation, the term has a special meaning; broadly, the making available by a corporation of its securities to the public. 3. Syn. for **allocation.**

distribution costs

The costs of selling, e.g. advertising, warehousing, delivery, etc.

diversified company

A company that is engaged in several distinctly different lines of business directly or through subsidiaries.

dividend

1. An amount of earnings declared by the board of directors for distribution to the shareholders of a corporation in proportion to their holdings, having regard for the respective rights of various classes of stock.

arrears of dividends	Unpaid dividends on cumulative preferred stock which must be paid before dividends can be paid on junior classes of stock.
cumulative dividends	Dividends, at a fixed annual rate, on preferred stock which, if not paid in one year, are carried forward as an additional priority of preferred shareholders in future income distributions.
extra dividend	A dividend paid in addition to the regular annual dividend.
passed dividend	The non-payment of a dividend which would normally have been paid in accordance with the corporation's established dividend policy.
stock dividend	A dividend payable by issue of shares of capital stock.
unpaid dividend	A dividend which has been declared, and is therefore a legal obligation but which has not been paid.
dividend	2. An amount distributed to the shareholders of a corporation upon liquidation. 3. An amount distributed to the creditors, pro rata, out of the net amount realized in a bankrupt estate. 4. A patronage return to the customers or members of a co-operative. 5. A rebate of life insurance premium based on favourable loss experience.
dividend coverage ratio	See **ratio analysis.**
donated share	See **share.**
donated surplus	See **surplus.**
dormant company	A corporation which is inactive except for compliance with the legal requirements pertaining to continuing existence. (Compare **operating company.**)
double account form of balance sheet	
double account system	See **balance sheet, form of.**
double entry bookkeeping	The system of bookkeeping, now in general use, in which every transaction is recorded both in one or more accounts as a debit and in one or more as a credit in such a manner that the total of the debit entries equals the total of the credit entries. (Compare **single entry bookkeeping.**)
doubtful account	
doubtful debt	An account or note receivable, the ultimate collectibility of which is uncertain. (Compare **bad debt.**)
down time	Time lost by machinery and equipment because of lack of business, material shortages, machine breakdowns, retooling or similar causes. (Compare **idle time.**)
downpayment	A part payment of the purchase price made at the time the contract is entered into.
draft	See **bill of exchange.**
draw-down	A charge against a deferred income tax credit account arising from an excess of the current liability for income taxes over the income tax expense for the year computed on an interperiod tax allocation basis.

37

drawings	Withdrawals of assets (usually cash or merchandise) from a business by a sole proprietor or partner.

E

E. & O. E.	(*abbr.*) Errors and omissions excepted. This notation is sometimes put on an invoice or statement of account to reserve the right to make corrections if errors are subsequently found.
earned income	A term used in income tax legislation; broadly, income from personal services rendered, the carrying on of business or rental income.
earned surplus	(*obs.*) Syn. for **surplus—retained earnings.**
earning power	The ability of an enterprise or security to earn. The term is usually applied to the present value of estimated future earnings.
earnings	1. A generic term used to mean income or profit. 2. (*colloq.*) Revenue.
earnings, statement of	Syn. for **statement, income.**
earnings per share	The portion of income for a period attributable to a share of issued capital of a corporation. The calculation of earnings per share is relevant only with respect to shares whose rights to participate in the earnings have no upper limit.
basic earnings per share	The amount of current earnings attributable to each common share outstanding during the period.
fully diluted earnings per share	The amount of current earnings per share reflecting the maximum potential dilution that would have resulted from conversions, exercises and other contingent issuances that would have decreased earnings per share or increased a loss per share.
primary earnings per share	(*U.S.*) The amount of current earnings per share attributable to each common share outstanding during the period, including common stock equivalents.
pro-forma earnings per share	The amount of current earnings per share reflecting transactions occurring subsequent to the end of the period and involving the issue of common shares.
supplementary earnings per share	(*U.S.*) A computation of earnings per share, other than primary or fully diluted earnings per share, which gives effect to conversions, etc., which took place during the period or shortly thereafter as though they had occurred at the beginning of the period (or date of issuance of the shares, if later).
economic life	The period during which a fixed asset can efficiently be kept in use. (Compare **physical life.**)

economic order quantity	That quantity at which the unit cost of placing the order is equal to the unit cost of carrying that quantity of material in storage.
economic unit	1. Any person, or group of persons with a common purpose, who engages in business transactions with others. 2. A group of business enterprises operating under common control where the financial statements could be consolidated.
EDP	Abbreviation for **electronic data processing.**
effective rate	The ratio of income realized to the sum invested. (Compare **nominal rate.**)
effectively controlled company	A corporation which is under the control of another corporation or person by some means other than through the ownership of a majority of the voting shares.
efficiency variance	See **variance** 2.
electronic data processing	See **data processing.**
eliminating entries	Adjustments in the preparation of consolidated or combined financial statements, made to prevent duplication due to intercompany transactions.
embezzlement	Misappropriation of assets in one's custody. Embezzlement restricted to cash is usually referred to as defalcation.
encumbrance	1. An expenditure commitment charged against a budget appropriation (chiefly in governmental accounting). 2. A charge upon real or personal property.
endowment fund	Property (often in the form of cash or investments acquired by gift or bequest) of a charitable, religious, educational, or other non-profit institution, the income from which is used for general or specific purposes according to the conditions attaching to the gifts, and the principal of which must be maintained intact or applied to the purposes of the fund.
engagement letter	A letter from a public accountant to a client outlining the scope of the accountant's responsibilities and the arrangements agreed upon with respect to an engagement.
entity concept entity theory	The view of the relationship between an accounting entity and its owners that regards the entity as a separate person, distinct and apart from its owners. (Compare **proprietary concept; proprietary theory.**)
entity value (of asset)	The value of an asset to the particular entity owning the asset as compared to the value of the asset to an outsider.
entry	A record, in a book of account or other accounting document, of the effect of an operation or transaction.
equity	1. The claim or right of proprietors or creditors to the assets of a business. 2. The residual interest of an owner or shareholder.

equity method
A basis of accounting for intercorporate investments whereby the investment is initially recorded at cost and the carrying value adjusted thereafter to show the investor's pro rata share of the post-acquisition earnings of the investee computed on a consolidated basis. (Compare **cost method.**)

equivalent units
The number of complete units that would have been produced if all the work performed during the period had been applied to units which were begun and finished during the period.

escalator clause
A clause inserted in a purchase or rental contract which permits, under specified conditions, upward adjustments of price or allowances.

escrow
An agreement whereby a deed, money or other property is deposited with a trustee to be held until certain conditions are fulfilled.

estate planning
The arrangement of an individual's affairs for the purpose of facilitating the passage of his assets to the beneficiaries of his estate, taking into account all of the allowances and benefits that tax and estate laws provide.

estimated cost system
See **cost accounting method.**

ex div. or **ex dividend**
The condition of shares whose quoted market price does not include a declared but unpaid dividend. This condition pertains after the record date and before the payment date of the dividend. (Compare **cum div.** or **cum dividend.**)

ex rights
The condition of securities whose quoted market price no longer includes the right to purchase new securities, such rights having expired or been retained by the vendor. (Compare **cum rights.**)

exception
(*obs.*) Syn. for **qualification.**

exchange
n. 1. The charge made by a bank for handling a bill of exchange drawn on another bank or on a branch of the same bank in another location. 2. An organized market for the purchase and sale of stocks or commodities.

executor
A person appointed by a testator to give effect to his will after his death. (Compare **administrator** 2.)

exhibit
A part of a financial statement. Sometimes the principal statements are called exhibits while the supplementary statements are called schedules.

expenditure
A disbursement, a liability incurred or the transfer of property for the purpose of obtaining goods or services. (Compare **disbursement; expense.**)

expense
A cost properly identifiable with the operations of a period or with revenues earned during that period or that is not identifiable with the operations or revenues of a future period or periods. (Compare **cost; expenditure; loss.**)

expense account
1. A ledger account in which expense amounts are entered.
2. An arrangement with an employer which allows an employee

to be reimbursed for certain costs incurred by him.

expired cost That portion of an expenditure whose benefit has been exhausted; an expense. (Compare **unexpired cost.**)

extendible bond See **bond** 1.

extra dividend See **dividend** 1.

extraordinary items Gains, losses and provisions for losses which result from occurrences the underlying nature of which is not typical of the normal business activities of the enterprise, are not expected to occur regularly over a period of years, and are not considered as recurring factors in any evaluation of the ordinary operations of the business.

F

face amount
face value Syn. for **par value.**

factor *n.* An agent; commonly used to describe an individual or corporation that buys receivables at a discount from another to provide the vendor with cash and/or to relieve the vendor of the risk of collecting the receivables.

factory expense Syn. for **overhead—factory overhead.**

factory ledger A subsidiary ledger in which manufacturing costs are assembled; a work-in-process ledger.

factory overhead
factory service See **overhead.**

factory supplies Syn. for **materials—direct materials.**

fair market value
fair value The price that would be agreed to in an open and unrestricted market between knowledgeable and willing parties dealing at arm's length who are fully informed and not under any compulsion to transact.

fair value pooling Syn. for **business combination, method of accounting for—new entity method.**

F.A.S. (*abbr.*) Free alongside. A condition of sale where the price of goods to be sold includes all charges until the goods are placed alongside the vessel (including a ship, railway car or other vehicle) in which they are to be shipped. (Compare **C. & F.; C. I. F.** and **F.O.B.**)

feasibility study An investigation of the advantages and disadvantages of a proposed course of action, e.g. advantages and disadvantages of using computer or data processing equipment instead of manual methods, or of using an alternative type of equipment over present equipment.

fiduciary accounting The accounting for the assumption and discharge of the responsibilities of a trustee.

field work	Work carried out by an auditor outside of his office, usually at the client's premises.
FIFO	(*abbr.*) See **cost allocation methods.**
financial accounting	That branch of accounting concerned with the classification, recording, analysis and interpretation of the overall financial position and operating results of an organization.
financial condition	Syn. for **financial position.**
financial expense	Expenses of an organization relating to the cost of financing its operations, as contrasted with expenses incurred for other particular purposes.
financial period	Syn. for **fiscal period.**
financial position	The state of affairs of an organization represented by the assets, liabilities and owners' equity at any specified time.
financial position, statement of	Syn. for **balance sheet.**
financial position form	See **balance sheet, form of.**
financial reporting	The communication of information by an organization to interested parties through financial statements.
financial statement	1. A balance sheet, income statement, statement of retained earnings, statement of changes in financial position, or any other formal accounting report. 2. A report comprising several accounting statements such as those in 1.
financing lease	See **lease.**
finished goods **finished stock**	Goods which have been manufactured or processed and are ready for sale.
first in, first out	See **cost allocation methods—FIFO.**
first mortgage	See **mortgage.**
fiscal period	The period for which financial statements are prepared; generally the fiscal year.
fiscal year	A period of approximately one year for which financial statements are regularly prepared. A fiscal year may consist of (1) twelve consecutive months or (2) 52 consecutive weeks with one extra day added to the last week or (3) 52 or 53 consecutive weeks.
fixed asset	A tangible long-term asset, such as land, building, equipment, etc., held for use rather than for sale. (Compare **capital asset** 1.)
fixed budget	See **budget.**
fixed capital	Investment in capital assets. (Compare **working capital.**)
fixed cost **fixed expense**	An indirect cost that remains relatively unchanged in total regardless of the volume of production or activity within a fairly

wide range of volume. (Compare **semi-variable cost; variable cost.**)

fixed price contract

A contract under which the contractor is to receive as payment a fixed amount stipulated in the contract. (Compare **cost-plus contract.**)

fixture

A part of fixed assets usually consisting of machinery or equipment attached to or forming a normal part of a building.

flat

(*colloq.*) Nil, particularly as to the balance of an account and, in the case of bonds, without accrued interest.

flexible budget

See **budget.**

floating charge

A general claim on the assets of a corporation, given as debt security, without attachment to specific assets.

flow chart

A graphic presentation of the movement in operational sequence of goods, documents or work flow, especially related to the operations of an organization.

flow-through basis

Syn. for **taxes payable basis.**

F.O.B.

(*abbr.*) Free on board. A condition of sale where the price of goods to be sold includes all charges until the goods are placed aboard the vessel (including a ship, railway car or other vehicle) in which they are to be shipped. (Compare **C.&F.; C.I.F.** and **F.A.S.**)

folio

The number of a page or of two facing pages which bear the same number.

foot

v. To add columns of figures. See also **crossfoot.**

forecast

An estimate of future events or conditions. (Compare **budget; projection.**)

foreign business corporation

A term in income tax legislation; broadly, a corporation incorporated in Canada which carries on its business operations and has its assets situated outside Canada.

foreign exchange

1. A transaction involving the exchange of currency of one country for currency of another country. 2. (*colloq.*) The currency of a foreign country. 3. See **rate of exchange.**

forfeited share

See **share.**

forward averaging

See **averaging.**

forward exchange contract

A contract for the purchase or sale of foreign exchange at a stipulated price on a specified future date.

franchise

A contractual privilege, often exclusive, granted by one person to another permitting the sale of a product, use of a trade name or provision of a service within a specified territory and/or in a specified manner.

fraud

A deliberate act of deception or manipulation with the specific intent of cheating or injuring another person or organization and providing illegitimate personal gains.

freight	1. A charge for transportation of goods. 2. The physical goods being transported.
freight-in	Freight paid by the purchaser on incoming shipments of goods and materials.
freight-out	Freight paid or allowed by the seller on shipments of goods and materials to customers.
front-end loading	The practice of some open-end investment companies of taking from the first year's instalments, the entire loading charge for shares to be purchased under a long-term plan. See **loading**.
full cost accounting **full costing**	1. The method of accounting whereby all costs of exploring for and developing oil and gas reserves within an area of interest are deferred, subject only to the limitation that costs attributable to developed reserves should not exceed their estimated present value. 2. Syn. for **cost accounting method—absorption costing**.
fully diluted earnings per share	See **earnings per share**.
fully funded pension plan	See **pension plan**.
functional accounting	A system of accounting whereby costs (and sometimes revenues) are allocated to each function or activity.
fund	*n*. 1. A self-balancing accounting entity set up to show capital or trust monies received for specific purpose(s), the income thereon, expenditures for the purpose(s) designated and the assets held against the capital of the fund. See **fund accounting**. 2. Assets (cash, investments, etc.) set aside for specific purposes. 3. A portion of capital or equity earmarked or designated for specific purposes or for specific interests. Used especially in life insurance accounting, e.g. participating policyholders' fund, shareholders' fund. *v*. To provide funds for a given purpose.
fund accounting	Accounting procedures in which a self-balancing group of accounts is provided for each accounting entity established by legal, contractual or voluntary action, especially in governmental units. Examples of the types of funds which are accounted for separately by governmental units are the capital fund, the current, revenue or general fund, the sinking fund, special activity funds, and trust funds. The accounts of each such entity will record the financial and other resources on the one hand and the liabilities and other credits on the other, together with the fund balance.
funded debt	Outstanding bonds or long-term notes.
funds	(*pl.*) Working capital (as used in the expression "source and application of funds").
funds statement	Syn. for **statement of changes in financial position** and **statement of source and application of funds**.
futures	Contracts to purchase or sell commodities, traded on an organized exchange, for future delivery.

G

GAAP	Abbreviation for **generally accepted accounting principles.**
GAAS	Abbreviation for **generally accepted auditing standards.**
gain	A monetary benefit, profit or advantage resulting from a transaction or group of transactions.
general account	See **balance sheet, form of—double account form.**
general accounting	Syn. for **financial accounting.**
general averaging	See **averaging.**
general expenses	Expenses not otherwise classified.
general insurance	See **insurance.**
general journal	The book of original entry in which are recorded those transactions or entries for which specialized journals have not been provided.
general ledger	A ledger comprising all asset, liability, proprietorship, revenue, and expense accounts, in the form of detailed, summary, or controlling accounts or a combination of these.
general price-level accounting	A method of accounting in which assets, liabilities, revenues and expenses are stated in terms of a single unit of measurement, usually the purchasing power of a monetary unit at the date of the current financial statements.
general purpose financial statement	A financial statement serving, as far as possible, the needs of all users.
generally accepted accounting principles	Those accounting principles which have been given formal recognition or authoritative support in any particular jurisdiction.
generally accepted auditing standards	Those auditing standards which have been given formal recognition or authoritative support in any particular jurisdiction.
GNE implicit price index	See **price index.**
going concern concept	The view that a business will continue in operation indefinitely. This concept is of special significance in the valuation of fixed and intangible assets for accounting purposes.
going concern value **going value**	The value of an asset or of net assets based on the assumption of continued use in the operations of the business, as distinct from market or liquidation value. (Compare **liquidation value; market value** 1.)
goods in process	Syn. for **work in process.**
goodwill	An intangible asset of a business when the business has value in excess of the sum of its net identifiable assets. Goodwill has

had a variety of definitions, some relating to the nature of the asset, others to its value. As to its nature, it has been said to fall into the three classes of commercial, industrial, and financial goodwill, which are the consequence of favourable attitudes on the part of customers, employees, and creditors, respectively. As to its value, the most common explanations emphasize the present value of expected future earnings in excess of the return required to induce investment. See also **consolidated goodwill.**

governmental accounting
That branch of accounting concerned with the principles, classification, recording, analysis and interpretation of the overall financial position and operating results of municipal, provincial, national and other governmental units.

gross
adj. The total without deductions, e.g. gross sales, gross revenue. (Compare **net.**)

gross margin
gross profit
The difference between cost and selling price; excess of net sales over the cost of goods sold.

gross profit ratio
See **ratio analysis.**

gross profit test
A test of the validity of the closing inventory figure(s) by comparing the gross profit ratio for the period with those of prior periods taking into consideration known changes in selling prices and costs of production.

group accounts
(Br.) The financial statements covering the business of a holding company and its subsidiary companies; the "group accounts" take the form of one or several sets of consolidated statements or a set consisting of the financial statements of each company in the group. See **consolidated financial statements.**

group depreciation
See **depreciation unit.**

guarantee
n. 1. A contract to perform the obligation or discharge the liability of another person if the latter fails to do so. 2. Syn. for **warranty.**

guaranteed investment certificate
A certificate showing that a deposit of a specified amount has been made at a trust company for a specified period of time, generally five years, and at a specified rate of interest. In ordinary circumstances, the certificate is not redeemable before maturity. (Compare **deposit certificate.**)

guarantor
A person who promises to perform the obligation or discharge the liability of another person if the latter fails to do so.

H

hardware
The physical equipment or devices forming a computer and peripheral equipment. (Compare **software.**)

hedge
v. To buy or sell commodity or foreign exchange futures for the

specific purpose of eliminating or restricting the risk involved in price fluctuations.

hidden reserve
Syn. for **secret reserve.**

hire-purchase agreement
A lease containing a purchase option.

historical cost
The total expenditures made by the owner to acquire title to an asset.

holdback
A portion of the progress payments called for under the terms of a contract which is not payable until the contract has been completed and the contractor has fulfilled his own financial obligations to subcontractors.

holding company
A corporation whose principal business is owning a controlling interest in the shares of one or more other corporations. (Compare **operating company; parent company.**)

holding gains
Increases in the value of assets or decreases in the value of liabilities occurring over a period of time and not resulting from actions of the owner.

holding losses
Decreases in the value of assets or increases in the value of liabilities occurring over a period of time and not resulting from actions of the owner.

horizontal analysis
See **ratio analysis.**

horizontal integration
The extension of activity by an organization in the same general line of business or expansion into supplementary, complementary or compatible products. (Compare **vertical integration.**)

horizontal business combination
See **business combination.**

human resources accounting
The identification, measurement and reporting of the investment by an organization in acquisition, training and retention of employees.

hypothecate
To pledge as collateral.

I

ideal capacity
See **capacity.**

idle capacity
See **capacity.**

idle time
Time lost by labour or machinery because of lack of business, material shortages, machine breakdowns, retooling or similar causes. (Compare **down time.**)

impairment of capital
See **capital impairment.**

imprest fund
A fund kept under the imprest system, e.g. imprest petty cash fund.

imprest system
A system for handling disbursements wherein a specified amount of cash or a bank balance is entrusted to an individual. The cash or bank balance is reimbursed from time to time for the exact amount of the disbursements from it on the basis of

the vouchers covering the disbursements. At any time, the cash on hand or the bank balance plus the disbursement vouchers not reimbursed should equal the amount of the fund.

improvement An expenditure made for the purpose of enhancing the utility of a fixed asset and which may be regarded as an addition to the cost of the property. (Compare **maintenance; repair.**)

imputed cost 1. That portion of the total cost of goods and services acquired in a lot or produced jointly that is allocated to an individual unit of goods or services. 2. A cost that is not recognized in conventional accounting records since it does not, of itself, result in dollar outlays, e.g. the computation of interest on ownership equity.

income 1. The excess of revenues over expenses for a period, usually referred to as "net income". See **accounting income; taxable income.** (Compare **revenue** 1.) 2. Revenue derived from investments and from incidental sources. 3. Revenue of an individual such as salary, interest, rent, etc.

income account 1. An account for a specified class of revenue. See **accounting** *n.* 1. 2. Syn. for **profit and loss account** 1.

income averaging See **averaging.**

income bond See **bond** 1.

income statement
income, statement of See **statement, income.**

incorporation The legal process of bringing a corporation into existence.

incremental analysis See **analysis.**

incremental cost Syn. for **marginal cost.**

independence A condition of mind and circumstance which permits an individual to apply unbiased judgment and objective consideration in arriving at an opinion or decision.

indirect cost An item of cost that cannot be reasonably identified with a specific unit of product or with a specific operation or other cost centre.

indirect labour The cost of labour expended which does not directly affect the construction or composition of the finished product of a manufacturing process.

indirect material See **material.**

indirect overhead See **overhead.**

information circular Under corporations and securities legislation, a document, accompanying the notice of a shareholders' meeting, prepared in connection with the solicitation of proxies by or on behalf of the management of the corporation. It contains information concerning the persons making the solicitation, election of directors, appointment of auditors and other particulars of matters to be acted upon at the meeting.

inner reserve In financial institutions, a provision which is not separately

	disclosed in the balance sheet because it has been either applied against an asset or grouped with liabilities and whose transfers from or to income account are not disclosed in the income statement.
input	1. The quantity of goods or services entering the production process. 2. Information introduced into a data processing system.
input/output analysis	See **analysis.**
insider	A person, as defined by corporate and securities legislation, who could be expected to be privy to information with respect to a corporation, e.ġ. directors, officers and major shareholders.
insider trading	Sales and purchases of the shares of a corporation by insiders.
insolvency	The inability of an individual or corporation to pay its debts as they become due. (Compare **bankruptcy.**)
inspector	1. A person appointed under corporations legislation to investigate the affairs and management of a corporation. 2. One of a number of persons, not exceeding five, appointed by creditors of a bankrupt to guide the trustee and to review and approve his accounts.
instalment	A portion of a debt divided into portions that become payable over a period of time.
instalment sale	A sale in which the price is to be settled by a series of payments over a period of time.
institutional investor	An institution which invests large sums in securities, e.g. insurance companies, pension funds, mutual funds.
instrument of incorporation	The document by which a body corporate is created. Depending on the Canadian jurisdiction, it may be articles of incorporation, letters patent or memorandum of association.
insurable interest	A person's interest in property or in another person's life of such a nature as to expose him to pecuniary loss or liability in the event of damage or destruction to the property or injury or death of that other person.
insurance	A contract under which one party (the insurer), in return for consideration (a premium), agrees to indemnify the other party (the insured) in the event of specified damage, loss or liability arising from the occurrence of certain events.
business interruption insurance	Insurance against continuing expenses and loss of earnings resulting from interruption of business caused by fire or other insured peril.
buy-out insurance	See **buy-out insurance.**
co-insurance	1. A stipulation in an insurance contract requiring the insured to maintain an agreed percentage of insurance to the value of the thing insured or, failing this, to contribute proportionately to his own loss. The percentages in common use are 80%,

	90% and 100%. 2. Joint underwriting of insurance.
general insurance	Insurance other than life insurance; e.g. fire, accident, medical, business interruption.
life assurance **life insurance**	Insurance in which the amount specified in the contract is payable on the death of the person covered by the contract.
reinsurance	A contract between insurers whereby one assumes part or all of the risk on an insurance contract issued by the other.
self-insurance	The assumption by an individual or a corporation of a risk which otherwise might have been covered by insurance.
insurance coverage	The nature and amount of risk insured in an insurance contract.
insurance fund	A fund of cash or investments set aside for self-insurance.
insured	*n.* 1. In general insurance, the party whose interests are covered by an insurance contract. 2. In the case of life insurance, the person whose life is covered by the contract.
intangible asset	A long-term or non-current asset that lacks physical substance, e.g. goodwill, patents, copyrights, trademarks, leaseholds, mineral rights.
integrated data processing	The co-ordination or combination of data processing operations so that duplicate data entry or processing steps are reduced or eliminated; commonly achieved through use of a computer.
intercompany eliminations	See **eliminating entries.**
intercompany profit	The excess of charges by one related company to another for services rendered or goods sold over and above their cost to the related group conceived as a unit.
interest coverage ratio	See **ratio analysis.**
interim audit	See **audit.**
interim certificates	Provisional certificates of shares, bonds, or other securities issued pending preparation of formal certificates or payment in full on instalment issues.
interim file	A file of working papers covering an interim audit.
interim report **interim statement**	A report or statement prepared as at any date or for a period ending on any date within the regular fiscal year.
internal audit	See **audit.**
internal auditor	An employee whose duty it is to audit all or part of the accounts and/or operations of the organization. See **auditor.**
internal check	A system of allocation of responsibility, division of work and methods of recording transactions whereby the work of an employee or group of employees is checked continuously by having to be in agreement with the work of others or by being correlated with the work of other employees. An essential feature is that no one employee or group of employees has

exclusive control over any transaction or group of transactions. (Compare **internal control.**)

internal control
The plan of organization and all the co-ordinated methods and measures adopted by management to safeguard assets, ensure the accuracy and reliability of accounting data, promote operational efficiency and maintain adherence to prescribed policies.

internal control questionnaire
A set of questions designed to identify controls and procedures in effect and to bring out any weaknesses that exist in the system of internal control.

interperiod tax allocation
See **tax allocation.**

inter-vivos trust
See **trust.**

intestate
A deceased who did not leave a will.

intraperiod tax allocation
See **tax allocation.**

inventory
1. An itemized list of goods; the annual or other periodic account of stock taken in a business; the articles that are inventoried. 2. Items of tangible property which are held for sale in the ordinary course of business, or are in the process of production for such sale, or are to be currently consumed in the production of goods or services to be available for sale.

inventory certificate
A letter of representation obtained by the auditor from the client, covering the method of taking inventory, the basis of valuation and the ownership of goods included in the inventory.

inventory control
The control of stock-in-trade by means of accounting controls, such as perpetual inventory records, and by means of physical controls, such as proper methods of buying, storing, issuing and periodic or continuous counting of inventories on hand.

investigation
A special examination conducted for a particular purpose. It may be more or less extensive than the regular annual audit. Examples are an examination of operating results over a term of years for a prospective purchase or in connection with an issue of securities; an examination of books, vouchers, etc., in connection with fraud; an examination on behalf of a bank, finance company or prospective investor.

investment
An expenditure to acquire property which yields, or is expected to yield, revenue or service; the property so acquired.

investment company
investment trust
A corporation engaged in the business of investing in securities.

   closed-end fund
   closed-end investment company
An investment company with fixed capital and no provision for redemption of shares at the option of shareholders.

   mutual fund
An investment company which sells equity units or shares to investors and is required to redeem them on short notice at their net asset value.

open-end fund **open-end investment** **company**	Syn. for **mutual fund.**
real estate investment **trust (REIT)**	An unincorporated trust, created under a trust deed, to operate as a mortgage and real estate financing intermediary.
invoice	*n.* A document prepared by the seller setting out the details of goods sold or services rendered to the purchaser including quantity, price, terms of payment, etc. (Compare **credit note; debit note.**)
I.O.U.	(*colloq.*) An informal document acknowledging a debt, setting out the amount of the debt and signed by the debtor.
issued capital	See **share capital.**
item depreciation	See **depreciation unit.**

J

job cost system **job order costing**	See **cost accounting method.**
joint account	1. An account or statement of a joint venture. 2. A bank account which may be drawn upon individually by two or more persons.
joint cost	The common cost of producing joint products.
joint products	Differing goods produced together in the course of the processing operations, the products being in such relationship that none can be designated as the major product. (Compare **by-product.**)
joint stock company	1. (*U.S.*) A business organization created by agreement between two or more parties rather than by incorporation. It is similar to a limited company except that each shareholder is personally liable for the company's debts. 2. (*Br.*) (*obs.*) Limited company.
joint venture	A business undertaking entered into by two or more parties, which terminates upon completion of the specified project.
journal	1. Any book of original entry, including the specialized journals such as the sales journal and cash journal, in addition to the general journal. 2. (*colloq.*) Syn. for **general journal.**
journal entry	An entry in a general journal.
journal voucher	A document supporting an entry in a general journal.
judgment sampling	See **sampling.**
junior security	Security that has a lower priority of claims on assets and/or income than certain other securities. (Compare **senior security.**)

K

kiting
The act of depositing in one bank account a cheque drawn on another bank account and recording only the deposit on the day of the transfer. This has the effect of covering a cash shortage on the day of the transfer by increasing the balance of the cash in bank in the account into which the cheque was deposited without a corresponding decrease in the account against when the cheque was drawn. (Compare **lapping.**)

L

land improvements
Expenditures incurred in the process of putting land into a usable condition; these expenditures may include clearing, grading, levelling, landscaping, paving and installing sewer, water and gas mains.

lapping
The act of fraudulently withholding cash receipts and covering up the deficiency by depositing subsequent receipts. The process continues indefinitely until restitution is made, it is discovered, or it is covered up by a fraudulent entry to an expense account. (Compare **kiting.**)

last in, first out
See **cost allocation methods—LIFO.**

lead time
The time required between the adoption and the initiation of a plan of operation or production to provide for the acquisition of the necessary materials and facilities.

lease
The conveyance of the right to use an asset by one person (the lessor) to another (the lessee) for a specified period of time in return for rent.

    financing lease
A lease which is essentially a method of financing the purchase of property. The term of the lease is closely related to the estimated economic life of the asset, certain ownership attributes rest with the lessee, and transfer of title to the lessee may occur at the termination of the lease. (Compare **operating lease.**)

    leasehold
An interest in real estate conveyed by one person to another for a specified period of time in return for rent.

    leasehold improvements
Additions, improvements or alterations made to leased property by the lessee.

    lease-option agreement
A lease which gives the lessee the option to purchase the property at a specified date at a stipulated price.

    leveraged lease
A financial arrangement in which a purchaser acquires an asset, to be leased to a third party, and pays for it partly with his own funds and partly with funds raised from lenders on the

	security of the leased asset. The term refers to the method by which an asset is acquired rather than to the form of the lease.
operating lease	A lease in which the lessor retains the usual attributes of ownership and title to the property at the termination of the lease. (Compare **financing lease.**)
sale and leaseback	The sale of an asset with the purchaser concurrently leasing the asset to the seller for a long term.
leasehold	See **lease.**
leasehold improvements	See **lease.**
lease-option agreement	See **lease.**
ledger	A book of final entry, either containing all the accounts including control accounts (general ledger), or containing all the accounts of a particular type or nature (subsidiary ledger).
letter of consent	A letter to a securities commission in which an auditor gives his consent to the publication of his report upon the financial statements contained in a prospectus.
letter of credit	A letter or document issued by a bank on behalf of a customer authorizing the person named therein to draw money to a specified amount from its branches or correspondents when the conditions set out in the document have been met.
letter of representation	A written declaration to an auditor from his client made in order to avoid misunderstanding as to the treatment of inventories, liabilities, receivables, fixed assets, depreciation or other accounting policies and their consistent application in the financial statements under review.
letter stock	(*U.S.*) Stock issued to an investor who gives an undertaking, usually by letter, to hold such stock for investment.
letters patent	See **instrument of incorporation.**
leverage	The relationship between the percentage change in profits accompanying a change in volume and the percentage change in volume itself (operating leverage); the relationship between the return to common shareholders earned with the use of borrowed funds and the cost of the borrowed funds (capital leverage). Capital leverage is favourable when funds are borrowed and reinvested or utilized to produce a rate of return exceeding the cost of the borrowing.
leveraged lease	See **lease.**
levy	*n.* Syn. for **assessment.**
liability	1. In general, a debt owed. 2. In accounting, the money value of an enforceable obligation that may be included as a credit balance in accordance with generally accepted accounting principles.
liability certificate	A letter of representation to an auditor from his client describing the client's direct and indirect liabilities, extraordinary commitments, and assets pledged as security for debts.

lien

The right given by law or contract to a person to have a debt or duty satisfied out of the property belonging to the person owing the debt or duty.

life assurance
life insurance

See **insurance**.

life tenant

A person whose interest in property is limited to the duration of his life. (Compare **remainderman**.)

LIFO

(*abbr.*) See **cost allocation methods**.

limited company

A corporation with share capital in which the liability of shareholders for debts of the corporation is limited to the amount of the capital for which they have subscribed. (Compare **company; corporation**.)

limited partnership

See **partnership**.

line-by-line consolidation

(*colloq.*) Syn. for **proportionate consolidation**.

line of credit

A declaration of intent whereby a lender or supplier states that until further notice it is prepared to extend credit up to a stated maximum amount, on certain terms and conditions, to a borrower or customer.

linear programming

An algebraic method for selecting the best or optimum solution from many possible alternatives.

liquid assets

Cash on hand and in bank and temporary investments readily convertible into cash, available for payment of current liabilities. (Compare **current asset; quick assets**.)

liquidating dividend

See **dividend** 2.

liquidation

1. The payment of a debt. 2. The conversion of assets into cash. 3. The winding-up of the affairs of an organization by settling with its debtors and creditors, and distributing any remaining assets to its owners or such other persons as designated in its charter or constitution.

liquidation value

The price which an asset might be expected to realize on a forced sale or on the winding-up of the business. (Compare **going concern value; market value** 1.)

liquidator

A person appointed to conduct the winding-up of the affairs of an organization.

liquidity

The convertibility of assets into ready cash. (Compare **solvency**.)

liquidity ratio

Syn. for **ratio analysis—acid test ratio**.

list price

The price as set out in a catalogue, register, etc., subject to trade and cash discounts.

listed securities

Securities admitted to trading privileges on a stock exchange.

loading

An amount included in an instalment contract to cover administrative and selling costs, interest, risk and other factors. Sometimes referred to as finance charges.

long-form report	A report, prepared by a public accountant at the conclusion of an engagement, containing such items as details of the items in the financial statements, statistical data, explanatory comments, recommendations to management or a description of the scope of the examination more detailed than the description found in the usual short-form report. The long-form report may or may not include an audit opinion. (Compare **short-form report.**)
long position	(*security and commodity brokerage*) The condition of a purchaser who is entitled to delivery of securities or commodities from a broker; such purchaser is said to be "long" those securities or commodities in the broker's account. (Compare **short position.**)
long-term asset	Long-term investments, fixed assets, intangible assets and other assets that are not current assets.
long-term liability	A liability which, in the ordinary course of business, will not be liquidated within one year or within the normal operating cycle where that is longer than a year.
loophole	(*colloq.*) An omission or ambiguity in the text of a statute or contract which allows the intent of the statute or contract to be evaded.
loss	1. The excess of expenses over revenues for a period. 2. A cost incurred or expired without return or benefit.
loss carry-over	See **carry-over.**
loss leader	(*colloq.*) An item which is sold at a lower than normal price in order to attract customers.
loss ratio	(*insurance*) The ratio of claims allowed to premiums earned in a period for a particular type of risk.
lower of cost and market	A method of valuing items of inventory or marketable securities, under which losses inherent in declines of market prices below cost are recognized in the period in which such losses become apparent.
lump-sum purchase	The acquisition of a group of assets for a total price which is not broken down by individual assets or classes of assets.

M

maintenance	The cost of keeping a property in efficient working condition. (Compare **improvement; repair.**)
management	1. The act of planning, directing and controlling the activities of an organization or project to enable it to reach its goals. 2. The persons who are involved in the management of an organization.
management accounting	That branch of accounting which provides information to assist management of an organization to make operational decisions. (Compare **financial accounting.**)

management audit See **audit.**

management by exception A management approach designed to focus attention on significant variations from expected results and on the analysis of these variations.

management by objective A management approach designed to focus on the definition and attainment of overall and individual objectives with the participation of all levels of management.

management consulting The investigation of management problems or the evaluation of operations for the purpose of suggesting improvements or solutions.

management information system A system designed to provide all levels of management with timely and reliable information required for planning, control and evaluation of performance.

management letter A letter written to a client by a public accountant dealing with matters of control which require consideration of the client, together with recommendations for improvement. See also **long-form report.**

manufacturing account (*obs.*) A ledger account in which the costs of making any or all of the products of a manufacturing business are summarized.

manufacturing expenses Expenses of an organization relating to the production of goods as contrasted with expenses incurred for other functions such as selling, administration and financing.

manufacturing statement See **statement, manufacturing.**

margin *n.* 1. A deposit with a broker in partial payment for a security or commodity to be bought. 2. The excess of the market value of collateral over the loan it secures. 3. See also **gross margin; gross profit.**

margin of safety The excess of sales over the break-even sales volume. It may be expressed as a ratio, in dollars, or other units.

marginal cost The amount by which total costs are increased by the last unit of output at any given volume of production.

marginal revenue The amount by which the total revenues are increased by the last unit of sales at any given volume of sales.

mark-down The reduction of a previously established selling price of goods for sale.

market
market price
market value 1. The prevailing or last quoted price under conditions applicable in the circumstances. (Compare **going concern value; liquidation value.**) 2. (*inventories*) Any one of:(a) Current replacement cost, by purchase or reproduction of normal quantities under normal conditions (b) Net realizable value (*q.v.*) (c) Net realizable value reduced by an allowance for normal profit margin. 3. (*commodities and securities*) The closing quotation on an established exchange.

marketable security A security which is capable of reasonably prompt conversion into cash.

mark-on
mark-up 1. The amount added to the cost of merchandise to arrive at the price at which it will be offered for sale. 2. An addition to a previously established selling price of goods for sale.

matching (of revenues and expenses) The process of correlating expenses and revenues in order to determine the net income of an accounting period.

material *n.* Goods used in the manufacturing process, either directly, such as raw materials, or indirectly, such as factory supplies.

direct material The cost of material that will form an integral part of the final product in a manufacturing process.

indirect material The cost of material that is necessary to the production of a manufacturing company's goods for sale but does not form part of the final product.

raw material A commodity acquired for the purpose of being consumed or changed in form in the manufacturing process.

materiality Significance. As a general rule, in the context of financial statements, materiality may be judged in relation to the reasonable prospect of an item's significance in the making of decisions by users.

matrix An array of figures and/or other mathematical symbols arranged in horizontal rows and vertical columns.

maturity The due date of a security or debt.

memorandum entry An explanatory notation in a book of account which does not change the balance in any account.

memorandum of association See **instrument of incorporation.**

merchandise 1. Commodities which are the object of trade or commerce. 2. Stock-in-trade.

merger See **business combination.**

mineral rights The right to take minerals, oil or gas from under the surface of land or sea.

minority interest 1. The equity of the shareholders who do not hold the controlling interest in a controlled company. 2. In consolidated financial statements, the equity in subsidiaries that is applicable to shares that are not owned by the parent company or by a consolidated subsidiary company.

minutes A record of the proceedings at a meeting.

mix *n.* (*colloq.*) The relative proportions of various items included in a group.

mixed costs Costs that include both fixed and variable elements.

modified accrual method A phrase of vague meaning used in municipal accounting to describe a variety of methods which include departures from the accrual basis of accounting.

monetary assets	See **monetary items.**
monetary items	Money and claims to money the value of which, in terms of the monetary unit, is fixed by contract or otherwise.
monetary liabilities	See **monetary items.**
money-purchase pension plan	Syn. for **pension plan—cost based pension plan.**
mortgage	A conveyance of property from one person (the mortgagor) to another (the mortgagee) as a security for the payment of a debt or the discharge of some other obligation, the security being redeemable on the payment or discharge of such debt or obligation.
chattel mortgage	A mortgage secured by chattel.
first mortgage	A mortgage having priority over all other mortgages on a property.
mortgage bond	See **bond** 1.
multinational company	A business enterprise with activities and invested capital in several countries.
multi-step income statement	That form of income statement which contains groupings of items in order to produce intermediate balances such as gross profit and operating profit. (Compare **single-step income statement.**)
mutual fund	See **investment company.**

N

national income accounting	The preparation and interpretation of overall economic statistics of a nation in financial statement form, measuring the total earnings of labour and property from the production of goods and services.
natural business year	A twelve month period ending on a date that is especially appropriate for the year end of a business, usually in a season of minimal business activity, when inventories and perhaps receivables may be expected to be relatively low.
natural growth asset	An asset whose value will increase through natural growth, e.g. a stand of timber, a herd of cattle.
negative assurance	A statement by an accountant or auditor to the effect that nothing has come to his attention in the course of his work which would give him reason to believe that the matters under consideration do not meet a given standard.
negative confirmation	See **confirmation.**
negative goodwill	(*colloq.*) The excess of the book value or fair value of the interest acquired in the net assets of a subsidiary company over the price paid by the controlling company for the shares in the subsidiary.

net	After all applicable deductions have been made. Examples of its use are net profit, i.e. profit after deduction of all related costs; net price, i.e. the price subject to no further discounts; net sales, i.e. sales less returned sales. (Compare **gross.**)
net assets	The excess of the book value of the assets of an organization over its liabilities. See **capital** 1.
net book value	The unexpired cost of an asset carried on the financial records of an organization.
net current assets	Syn. for **working capital.**
net income	Syn. for **income** 1.
net-of-tax method	See **tax allocation—interperiod tax allocation.**
net realizable value	Estimated selling price in the ordinary course of business less reasonably predictable costs of completion and disposal.
net worth	See **capital** 1; **net assets; shareholders' equity.**
network analysis	See **analysis.**
new entity method	See **business combination, method of accounting for.**
NIFO	(*abbr.*) See **cost allocation methods.**
no par value stock	Shares of capital stock which have no nominal or par value.
nominal account	An account for revenue, income, expense, loss or income distribution. (Compare **real account.**)
nominal owner	The person who holds title to an asset on behalf of the beneficial owner.
nominal rate	The contract interest or dividend rate as related to par or face value or, in the case of no par value shares, the stated value of an investment. (Compare **effective rate.**)
non-arm's length	*adj.* Converse of **arm's length.**
non-contributory pension plan	See **pension plan.**
non-cumulative share	See **share.** See also **capital stock.**
non-cumulative stock	See **capital stock.**
non-current asset	Syn. for **long-term asset.**
non-ledger assets	Assets omitted from financial statements because of practice or regulations, e.g. the non-admitted assets of life insurance companies.
non-profit organization	An organization formed for social, educational or philanthropic purposes in which there is normally no transferable ownership interest and from which the members or contributors do not receive any economic gain.
note payable	A liability in the form of a promissory note. Generally used in the plural to refer to both drafts and notes payable and to distinguish them from open accounts payable. See **bill payable.**

note receivable	An asset in the form of a promissory note. Generally used in the plural to refer to both drafts and notes receivable and to distinguish them from open accounts receivable. See **bill receivable**.
notes to financial statements	Explanatory or supplementary information appended to and forming an integral part of financial statements.
nothings	(*colloq.*) An income tax term; broadly, intangible assets such as goodwill.

O

obsolescence	The condition of becoming out-of-date, obsolete, or useless as a result of new discoveries, improvements, or changes in consumer demand. (Compare **depreciation**.)
off-balance-sheet financing	(*colloq.*) A form of financial arrangement associated with some leveraged leases in which the lender of the funds agrees to look solely to the lessee and the value of the leased asset for repayment of the debt. In the event of default by the lessee, the lender has no recourse to the lessor.
offering circular	Syn. for **prospectus**.
officer	Any person in a corporation on whom executive authority has been conferred by legislation, by-law or resolution of the board of directors.
offset	*v.* To reduce by applying opposites against each other, e.g. an account payable can be offset against an account receivable from the same person.
on account	1. In partial payment. 2. On credit terms, rather than for cash.
one-write system	A system of bookkeeping in which all records, including original documents, are produced in one operation by the use of reproductive paper and special equipment which provides for proper alignment of the documents being processed.
open account	1. Any account which has a balance. 2. A credit term indicating an unsecured amount owing or receivable.
open-end	*adj.* Relating to the capital structure of an organization where shares or units of participation are not transferable and may be redeemed at the sole option of the shareholder or unitholder. (Compare **closed-end**.)
open-end fund **open-end investment** **company**	Syn. for **investment company—mutual fund**.
open-item file	A file of source documents serving as a ledger; open items, at any time, represent the account balance, e.g. a file of unpaid sales invoices serving as an accounts receivable ledger.
opening entry	The first entry or one of a series of entries in the books, setting

up assets, liabilities, and capital, e.g. on the formation of an organization.

operating   An adjective of imprecise meaning referring to either the principal activities of an organization as opposed to secondary or ancillary activities or its ordinary activities as opposed to non-recurring or extraordinary transactions.

operating company   A corporation actively engaged in business. (Compare **dormant company; holding company.**)

operating cycle   The time period between the acquisition of raw materials or merchandise and the recovery of cash from the related sale.

operating lease   See **lease.**

operating leverage   See **leverage.**

operating ratio   1. The percentage of total operating costs (cost of goods sold plus operating expenses) to total operating revenue. 2. In the plural ("operating ratios"), the ratios of the various items in an income statement to net sales.

operating statement   Syn. for **statement, income.**

operational audit   Syn. for **audit—management audit.**

operations research   The scientific analysis of an organization's operations and the application of scientific techniques, often in the form of mathematical formulas or models, to solving operating problems or improving operating efficiency.

opinion   See **auditor's opinion.**

opportunity cost   The value of benefits sacrificed in selecting a course of action among alternatives; the value of the next best opportunity foregone by deciding to do one thing rather than another.

option   The right of executing or renouncing a transaction within a specified period on agreed terms.

ordinary creditor   See **creditor.**

ordinary stock   Syn. for **capital stock—common stock.**

organization chart   A graphic presentation of the functional and procedural relationships, the lines of authority and responsibility, within an organization.

organization expense   A cost incurred in the formation or incorporation of an organization, including legal, accounting and registration fees.

original cost   Syn. for **historical cost.**

original entry   The first accounting record of a transaction.

out-of-pocket cost   1. An expense incurred for a third party and for which reimbursement may be sought. (Compare **allowance** 3.)
2. That portion of the total cost of a particular project which must be met through the outlay of cash, as opposed to imputed cost.

output   1. The quantity of goods or services produced. 2. Information produced by a data processing system.

outstanding
1. Uncollected (accounts or bills receivable). 2. Unpaid (liabilities). 3. Uncleared (cheques). 4. Unredeemed (capital stock.) 5. Unfilled (orders).

overabsorb
To charge estimated overhead to production in excess of actual overhead. (Compare **underabsorb**.)

overabsorbed burden
overapplied overhead
See **overhead**.

overdraft
The excess of withdrawals over the amount available in an account such as a bank account or an appropriation account.

overhead
Expenses which are incurred to produce a commodity or render a service, but which cannot conveniently be attributed to individual units of production or service.

   absorbed burden
   applied overhead
Overhead costs that have been allocated or apportioned to a product or activity.

   direct overhead
Overhead costs which are traceable to the specific part of the organization which is the focus of attention.

   factory overhead
   factory service
All production costs other than direct material and direct labour costs. These terms include all costs necessary to the operation and maintenance of the plant including wages of foremen, building and machinery upkeep, depreciation, light, heating, repairs, insurance, taxes, etc.

   indirect overhead
Overhead costs which are not traceable to the specific part of the organization which is the focus of attention.

   overabsorbed burden
   overapplied overhead
The amount by which overhead costs applied exceed actual overhead.

   underabsorbed burden
   underapplied overhead
The amount by which actual overhead costs exceed overhead costs applied.

over-the-counter
adj. Relating to transactions in securities or commodities not listed on an established exchange.

owners' equity
See **capital 1; net assets; shareholders' equity.**

P

paid-in surplus
Syn. for **surplus—contributed surplus.**

paid-up capital
See **share capital.**

paper profit
(*colloq.*) An unrealized profit, e.g. appreciation in market value of securities held.

par value
The nominal or face value of a security.

parent company	A corporation which controls one or more other corporations through ownership of a majority of the shares carrying the right to elect at least a majority of the members of the board of directors. Use of the term is usually restricted to cases where the controlling corporation is a limited company. (Compare **holding company; subsidiary company.**)
partially funded pension plan	See **pension plan.**
participating share	See **share.** See also **capital stock.**
participating stock	See **capital stock.**
partnership	The relationship which exists between persons carrying on a business in common with a view to profit. This term does not apply to the relationship which exists between members of a corporation.
limited partnership	A partnership in which some of the partners have their liability for the debts of the partnership limited to their contributed capital.
passed dividend	See **dividend** 1.
past service pension cost	See **pension costs.**
past service pension liability	See **pension costs.**
patent	The exclusive right granted under *The Patent Act* (Canada) to make, use and sell an invention for a period of seventeen years.
patronage dividend **patronage refund** **patronage return**	A distribution paid to customers, based on the volume of business done with each customer over a period.
pay-as-you-go	(*colloq.*) A method of accounting where expenses are recognized at the time of disbursement. Although the term could embrace any application of the cash basis of accounting to disbursements, its use is usually limited to areas such as fixed asset, income tax and pension accounting.
payback period	The estimated period of time required for the cash flow from an investment to return the original cost of the investment.
payroll	1. The book, sheet, or other record on which are listed the names of employees and the amounts payable to them as salaries or wages at a given time, with particulars as to rate of pay and deductions. 2. The total amount payable to employees at a given time or for a given period.
pension	A stipend paid to a retired employee or his beneficiaries.
pension benefits	The pensions and any other payments to which employees or their beneficiaries may be entitled under a pension plan.
pension costs	The cost to an employer of providing pension benefits.
current service pension cost	The pension cost which relates to an employee's period of employment after a pension plan becomes effective.

past service pension cost	The pension cost which relates to an employee's period of employment before a pension plan became effective.
past service pension liability	The present value of the cost of unpaid past service pension benefits.
pension fund	The pool of cash, investments, and other assets set aside for the payment of pensions.
pension plan	An arrangement, contractual or otherwise, by which a program is established to provide for the payment of pensions.
benefit based pension plan	A plan under which pension benefits are determined as a function of years of service and earnings. (Compare **cost based pension plan.**)
contributory pension plan	A plan where the costs are shared between the employee and the employer.
cost based pension plan	A plan under which pension benefits are determined as a function of accumulated contributions. (Compare **benefit based pension plan.**)
defined contribution pension plan	Syn. for **cost based pension plan.**
fully funded pension plan	A plan under which the pension fund is sufficient to provide for the pension benefits which have accrued to date.
money-purchase pension plan	Syn. for **cost based pension plan.**
non-contributory pension plan	A plan where the costs are borne by the employer.
partially funded pension plan	A plan in which the pension fund is not sufficient to provide for the pension benefits which have accrued to date.
unfunded pension plan	A plan under which no pension fund is set up.
unit benefit pension plan	Syn. for **benefit based pension plan.**
percentage-of-completion method	A method of accounting which recognizes income proportionately with the degree of completion of goods or services under a contract. (Compare **completed contract method.**)
period costs	Costs charged as expense in the period in which they are incurred and not included in inventory valuation. (Compare **product costs.**)
periodic inventory	A system of accounting for inventory where stock on hand is determined by physical inventory. (Compare **perpetual inventory.**)
permanent asset	Syn. for **capital asset** 1.
permanent capital	The portion of owners' equity that, by statute or agreement, is

not to be withdrawn or distributed in the ordinary course of events.

permanent differences

Differences between accounting income and taxable income which arise from including in accounting income certain expenses and losses or certain revenues and gains that will never be included in the computation of taxable income, or vice versa. (Compare **timing differences.**)

permanent file

The file of working papers containing information required for reference in successive audits of a particular organization, as distinguished from working papers applicable only to a particular year.

perpetual inventory

A system of accounting for inventory where a continuous record is kept of the flow of merchandise and/or materials and of the stock on hand. (Compare **periodic inventory.**)

person

A human being or corporation having rights and duties before the law.

personal account

1. An account with a debtor or a creditor. 2. A proprietor's or partner's drawing or current account.

personal corporation

A term in income tax legislation; broadly, an investment corporation owned by an individual or the members of a family.

personal financial statements

Financial statements of an individual or family; usually limited to a statement of assets and liabilities.

PERT

(*abbr.*) Program evaluation and review technique. A method of network analysis in which three time estimates are made for each activity—the optimistic time, the most likely time and the pessimistic time—and which gives an expected completion date for the project within a probability range. (Compare **Critical Path Method.**)

PERT/cost

The integration of cost estimates on a PERT network.

petition

(*bankruptcy*) A request to the court by a creditor or a group of creditors that the debtor be declared bankrupt.

petty cash

Cash kept on hand or in a special bank account as a convenience for making small payments.

physical inventory

An inventory determined by actual count, weight, or measurement.

physical life

The period of time in which a fixed asset is capable of providing a service irrespective of obsolescence and excessive maintenance costs. (Compare **economic life.**)

piecemeal opinion

See **auditor's opinion.**

plant

All or any of the tangible fixed property of an industrial organization including land, buildings, machinery and equipment.

pledge

n. A promise to contribute to a charitable or non-profit organization.

pooling of interests method See **business combination, method of accounting for.**

portfolio investments All long-term investments in companies which are not subsidiaries, effectively controlled companies or corporate joint ventures.

positive confirmation See **confirmation.**

post *v.* To transfer an amount to a ledger from a book of original entry or from a source document.

post-balance sheet event Syn. for **subsequent event.**

post-closing trial balance The trial balance of the general ledger accounts taken after all revenue and expense accounts have been closed.

posting *n.* The entry or amount posted in an account.

postulate See **accounting postulates.**

PPBS (*abbr.*) Planning, programming and budgeting system. (Used chiefly in government.) A management system concerned with the planning and control of resources in an organization to ensure that they are employed effectively to meet the organization's objectives. It emphasizes the definition of organizational objectives, selection of optimum programs for meeting these objectives, translation of planning and programming decisions into resource requirements and measurement of results (benefits) against resources used.

practice A professional partnership's or individual's clientele *in toto,* or his business.

pre-audit An examination performed before proceeding with a commitment, expenditure, payment, or other specified transaction, e.g. examination of contracts, purchase orders, appropriations, by-law requirements, and invoices, before payment of accounts.

pre-emptive right The right sometimes granted in corporations legislation or instruments of incorporation which entitles shareholders of a given class to subscribe for their pro rata share of any new issues of shares of the same class.

preferred creditor See **creditor.**

preferred share See **share.** See also **capital stock.**

preferred stock See **capital stock.**

preliminary expense (*obs.*) 1. Organization expense. 2. More broadly, a general term for organization, development, and other pre-production expenses.

preliminary prospectus See **prospectus.**

premium 1. The amount by which the selling price of a security exceeds its par value. (Compare **discount** *n.* 2.) 2. The consideration payable for the purchase of insurance protection or for an annuity contract.

prepaid expense

1. A short-term expense prepayment; an expenditure, other than an outlay for inventory or a capital expenditure, which is expected to yield its benefits in the near future and meanwhile is carried forward to be charged to expense in the near future. (Compare **deferred charge** 1.) 2. Balance of amounts paid for services not yet received from the payee and which meanwhile is carried forward to be charged to expense in future years. (Compare **deferred charge** 2.)

present value

Discounted value, assuming a given rate of interest and a given period of time.

price index

An indicator, derived by aggregating sets of representative unit prices with an appropriate weighting base, which measures changes in price levels over time. Price indexes are stated in terms of a base point of time where the price level is arbitrarily set at 100.

consumer price index

An index measuring changes in prices of retail goods and services purchased by the public.

GNE implicit price index

Gross national expenditure implicit price index. An index measuring changes in prices for all final expenditures on goods and services produced in the domestic economy.

wholesale price index

An index measuring changes in prices of commodities sold by producers and distributors to retailers.

price-level accounting

See **general price-level accounting.**

price maintenance

The action of a manufacturer, wholesaler or jobber who induces his retailers to sell his products to the public at not less than a specified price.

price variance

See **variance** 2.

primary distribution

The distribution to the public of securities issued by a corporation and not previously distributed to the public. (Compare **secondary distribution.**)

primary earnings per share

(*U.S.*) See **earnings per share.**

primary issue

An issue of securities being offered in primary distribution. (Compare **secondary issue.**)

prime cost

The direct cost of production, i.e. direct labour and direct material.

prime costing

See **cost accounting method.**

prime rate

The interest rate charged by a bank on loans to its preferential borrowers.

principal

1. A sum on which interest is earned or paid. 2. Syn. for **corpus.** 3. A person employing another person (the agent) to make contracts on its behalf with third persons.

principle

See **accounting principles.**

prior period adjustment

A gain or loss specifically identified with and directly related to the business activities of particular prior periods, not attributable to economic events occurring subsequent to the date of the financial statements for such prior periods, depending primarily on decisions or determinations by persons other than management or owners, and not reasonably estimable prior to such decisions or determinations. (Compare **correction of error.**)

private company
1. A limited company classified as a private company by virtue of the provisions of corporate legislation and its instrument of incorporation. 2. (*colloq.*) A limited company whose shares are not listed on a recognized stock exchange or otherwise available to the public investor.

private corporation
A term in income tax legislation; broadly, a private company.

private ledger
A ledger in which selected confidential accounts are kept, these accounts usually being represented in the general ledger by a controlling account.

procedural audit
See **audit.**

procedure manual
A detailed description for an organization or a department, function or activity setting out the authority and responsibilities of the various positions and the methods and detailed procedures by which activities are carried out, including examples of forms, reports, etc. (Compare **accounting manual.**)

proceeds of distribution
The net amount of cash received by an issuer from the sale of securities.

process cost system
process costing
See **cost accounting method.**

product costs
Costs associated with the product and thus included in inventory valuation. (Compare **period costs.**)

production method
See **depreciation method.**

profit
n. 1. Syn. for **income** 1. 2. The excess of the proceeds of the sale of an asset over its book value.

profit and loss account
1. The ledger account to which the balances of the revenue, income, expense, and loss accounts at the end of an accounting period are transferred, to show the net difference as the net income or net loss for the period. 2. (*Br.*) (a) Retained earnings. (b) The combined statement of income and retained earnings.

profit and loss statement
profit and loss, statement of
Syn. for **statement, income.**

profit centre
A unit of a business that is accountable for specific revenues and costs.

profit-sharing plan
1. A plan under which an employer makes available to employees special current or deferred sums, based on the net income of the business, in addition to normal remuneration. 2. Under income tax legislation, the term has a special meaning.

pro-forma

adj. A term applied to a financial statement drawn up after giving effect to stated assumptions or contractual commitments which have not yet been completed.

pro-forma earnings per share

See **earnings per share.**

program

n. 1. A definite plan to be followed in carrying out a procedure. 2. (*auditing*) See **audit program.** 3. The complete sequence of machine instructions and routines necessary to carry out a task on a computer.

program budgeting

See **PPBS.**

progress billing

An interim billing based upon partial completion of a contract.

progress payment

An interim payment based upon partial completion of a contract.

projection

An estimate of future events or conditions based on the present position and recent trends. (Compare **budget; forecast.**)

promissory note

An unconditional promise in writing made by one person to another, signed by the maker, promising to pay on demand or at a fixed or determinable future time, a sum certain in money to or to the order of a specified person or to bearer.

proportionate consolidation

A presentation of the financial statements of any investor-investment relationship, whereby the investor's pro rata share of each asset, liability, income item and expense item is reflected in the financial statements of the investor under the various balance sheet and income statement headings.

proposal

(*bankruptcy*) A scheme for extension of time and/or reduction or rearrangement of debt put forward to creditors by a debtor.

proprietary concept
proprietary theory

The view of the relationship between an accounting entity and its owners that regards the entity simply as the agent of its owners. (Compare **entity concept; entity theory.**)

prospectus

Under corporations and securities legislation, a document issued by a corporation in connection with an issue of securities. It contains information concerning the securities, a description of the corporation's business, names of its officers and directors, financial data and other pertinent facts.

preliminary prospectus

A document filed with a securities commission in advance of a final prospectus, the information in which is incomplete or subject to amendment.

protective covenant

A clause in a bond indenture placing restrictions on the operations of the borrower for the safeguarding of the lenders' interests.

provision

An estimated expense; a charge for a diminution in value of an asset or for an estimated or accrued liability.

proxy statement

(*U.S.*) Syn. for **information circular.**

public accountant	1. A person who offers accounting services to the public for reward. 2. A meaning given by a particular statute.
public accounting	1. The profession engaged in by public accountants, consisting principally of the investigation or audit of accounting records leading to the preparation of or reporting on financial statements. 2. A meaning given by a particular statute.
public company	1. A limited company which is not a private company. 2. (*colloq.*) A limited company whose shares are available to the public investor.
public corporation	A term in income tax legislation; broadly, a public company.
purchase book purchase journal	A book of original entry in which purchases on credit terms are recorded.
purchase discrepancy	The difference between the cost of the shares to an acquiring corporation and its equity in the net assets of the acquired corporation at the date of acquisition. (Compare **consolidated goodwill**.)
purchase method	See **business combination, method of accounting for.**
purchase order	A form used to place an order for goods or services with a supplier.

Q

qualification	A statement in an auditor's report setting forth a limitation or modification of his opinion.
qualified opinion qualified report	See **auditor's opinion.**
qualifying share	See **share.**
quantity discount	See **discount** *n.* 1.
quantity variance	See **variance** 2.
quasi-reorganization	A voluntary and informal reorganization, not requiring court approval, carried through with the consent of the shareholders. (Compare **recapitalization; refinancing; reorganization.**)
quick assets	(*colloq.*) Cash on hand and in bank, marketable securities held temporarily, accounts receivable maturing within the normal term of credit, short-term trade bills receivable. (Compare **current asset; liquid assets.**)
quick ratio	(*colloq.*) Syn. for **ratio analysis—acid test ratio.**
quoted market value	See **market value** 3.

R

random access	See **access.**
random number sampling	See **sampling.**

random sampling	See **sampling.**
rate of exchange	The price at which the currency of one country may be bought or sold in the currency of another country.
rate variance	See **variance** 2.
ratio analysis	The study of financial condition and performance through ratios derived from items in the financial statements.
acid test ratio	The ratio of the total cash, accounts receivable and marketable securities included in current assets to current liabilities.
current ratio	The ratio of current assets to current liabilities.
dividend coverage ratio	The ratio of the net income to dividends.
gross profit ratio	The ratio of gross profit to net sales.
horizontal analysis	The study of the behaviour of items in the financial statements over two or more fiscal periods.
interest coverage ratio	The ratio of net income before interest on long-term liabilities and income taxes to interest on long-term liabilities.
liquidity ratio	Syn. for **acid test ratio.**
quick ratio	(*colloq.*) Syn. for **acid test ratio.**
vertical analysis	The study of relationships existing among the items in the financial statements for a single fiscal period.
working capital ratio	Syn. for **current ratio.**
raw material	See **material.**
reacquired share	Syn. for **share—acquired share.**
real account	An account for any asset, liability or equity interest. (Compare **nominal account.**)
real estate	Land and improvements, including buildings, standing timber, orchard trees, etc.
real estate investment trust (REIT)	See **investment company.**
realization account	An account sometimes used in the liquidation of an estate or business, in which the amounts realized on sale of the assets are offset against the book values of the assets, thus showing the profit or loss on realization.
realization and liquidation, statement of	See **statement of realization and liquidation.**
realized income **realized profit**	A term of imprecise meaning used to describe the income or profit arising from a completed transaction which has produced either assets of a known monetary value or, in a more restricted sense, liquid assets.
rebate	A price allowance or price reduction.

recapitalization	An adjustment in the capital structure of a corporation involving changes in the nature and amounts of the various classes of shares and other components of shareholders' equity; asset carrying values in the accounts remain unchanged. (Compare **quasi-reorganization; refinancing; reorganization.**)
receipt	1. The act of receiving money or merchandise. 2. The amount of money or merchandise received. 3. A signed acknowledgement of the receipt of money or merchandise.
receipts and disbursements, statement of	See **statement of receipts and disbursements.**
receiver	A person appointed by a court or by a creditor to take charge of property pending final disposition of the matter before the court or payment in full of the debt owed to the creditor.
receivership	The legal status of a debtor for whom a receiver has been appointed.
receiving order	(*bankruptcy*) A court order issued following a successful petition by a creditor or creditors establishing that the debtor is bankrupt.
reconciliation **reconciliation statement**	Any statement accounting for the differences between two related records, e.g. the statement drawn up to account for the difference between a bank balance as reflected in the books of the bank and the balance of the same account as reflected in the books of the bank's customer.
record	*v.* To enter a transaction in accounting records.
record date	The date selected by the board of directors of a limited company for identification of shareholders for making a distribution of some kind, e.g. dividends, issue of rights.
records	Syn. for **accounting records.**
red-herring prospectus	(*colloq.*) Syn. for **prospectus—preliminary prospectus.**
redeemable share	See **share.** See also **capital stock.**
redeemable stock	See **capital stock.**
redemption	The purchase of securities by the issuer at a time and price stipulated in the terms of the securities.
redemption fund	(*obs.*) Syn. for **sinking fund.**
redemption price **redemption value**	The price payable on redemption of securities.
reducing balance method	Syn. for **depreciation method—diminishing balance method.**
refinancing	An adjustment in the capital structure of a corporation, involving changes in the nature and amounts of the various classes of debt and, in some cases, capital as well as other components of shareholders' equity; asset carrying values in the accounts remain unchanged. (Compare **quasi-reorganization; recapitalization; reorganization.**)

refunding	The exchange of a currently maturing liability for one which matures at some more distant date in the future.
registrar	An employee or agent of a corporation responsible for the maintenance of its shareholders' and bondholders' records. (Compare **transfer agent.**)
regression analysis	See **analysis.**
reinsurance	See **insurance.**
related company	Syn. for **affiliated company** or **associated company.**
remainderman	A person who is entitled to the remaining interest in a property after a life tenancy expires. (Compare **life tenant.**)
renewal accounting	An accounting procedure in which no charge for expense is made for a fixed asset until replacement occurs, the cost of the replacement rather than the cost of the original asset then being charged to expense. (Compare **depreciation accounting; retirement accounting.**)
rent roll	A record of rents receivable kept by an owner of property or his agent.
reorganization	A court-approved realignment of the capital structure of a corporation, in which debt holders and the various classes of shareholders give up some (or all) of their rights and claims upon the corporation, the assets of the corporation are written down to values that are more realistic under current operating conditions, and the retained earnings account is begun anew. (Compare **quasi-reorganization; recapitalization; refinancing.**)
repair	The cost of replacement of parts or other restoration of plant or machinery, designed to restore normal working efficiency. (Compare **improvement; maintenance.**)
replacement	Substitution of one asset for another of the same kind, usually the substitution of a new unit of plant for an old unit.
replacement accounting	Syn. for **renewal accounting.**
replacement cost **replacement value**	The current cost of replacing an asset with another which will render similar services.
report form (of statement)	See **balance sheet, form of.**
reporting standards	Criteria for evaluating the fairness of financial statement presentation.
representation letter	See **letter of representation.**
reproduction cost	The current cost of reproducing an asset in substantially identical form.
repurchased share	Syn. for **share—acquired share.**
requisition	A written order by one department to another for specified articles, services, or cash.
reservation	See **auditor's opinion—adverse opinion; denial of opinion; piecemeal opinion; qualified opinion.**

reserve	1. An amount appropriated from retained earnings or other surplus, at the discretion of management or pursuant to the requirements of a statute, the instrument of incorporation or by-laws of a company or a trust indenture, or other agreement, for a specific or general purpose such as future decline in inventory values, general contingencies, future plant extension, and redemption of stocks or bonds. The reserve indicates that an undivided or unidentified portion of the net assets, in a stated amount, is being held or retained for general or specific purposes. 2. Under income tax legislation, the term has several special meanings.
reserve fund	A pool of designated assets, usually cash and investment securities, earmarked for a specified purpose, e.g. sinking fund for bond redemption.
residual value	1. The value remaining to an asset which has served its economically useful life consisting of salvage value and scrap value. 2. Syn. for **amortized value.**
responsibility accounting	A system of accounting whereby costs (and sometimes revenues) are allocated to each area of managerial responsibility.
responsibility costing	Syn. for **responsibility accounting.**
rest account	The general reserve account of a bank.
retail method	A method of estimating inventory value based on recording purchases both at cost and at selling price. The ratio of cost to selling price is applied to the book inventory at selling price to determine estimated cost.
retained earnings	See **surplus.**
retained earnings, statement of	See **statement of retained earnings.**
retirement accounting	An accounting procedure in which no charge to expense is made for a fixed asset until it is removed from service, the original cost being charged against operations in the year in which the asset is retired. (Compare **depreciation accounting; renewal accounting.**)
retractable bond	See **bond** 1.
return	*n.* 1. A statement of information required by governmental bodies from individuals or corporations. 2. The profit resulting from an investment (return on investment) or from a transaction (e.g. return on sales).
return on investment (ROI)	See **return** 2.
returns	Items of merchandise returned by a purchaser to the vendor.
revaluation reserve **revaluation surplus**	(*obs.*) Syn. for **appraisal increase credit.**
revenue	1. The gross proceeds from the sale of goods and services (generally after deducting returns, allowances and discounts), gains from the sale or exchange of assets (other than

stock-in-trade), interest and dividends earned on investments and other realized increases in owners' equity in a business except those arising as a result of capital contributions and adjustments. (Compare **income.**) 2. (*government accounting*) The gross proceeds from taxes, licences, duties and sources other than borrowing.

revenue and expenditure, statement of

See **statement of revenue and expenditure.**

revenue and expense, statement of

Syn. for **statement, income.**

revenue expenditure

1. An expenditure that is properly chargeable against revenue of a business. 2. (*government accounting*) An expenditure that is paid out of current operating revenue.

reverse split

(*colloq.*) Syn. for **consolidation** (of shares).

reverse takeover

An acquisition in which the former owners of the acquired company receive as consideration sufficient shares in the acquiring company to obtain control.

reversing entry

An entry made at the beginning of an accounting period to bring into the accounts for the period any deferred or accrued amounts set up at the end of the preceding period.

revolving fund

A fund provided for a particular purpose which is periodically replenished either from operations or by transfers from other funds, e.g. a working capital fund provided to finance branch or departmental operations; an imprest petty cash fund.

right

(*colloq.*) Syn. for **share right.**

ROI

Abbreviation for **return on investment.**

roll-over

A term in income tax legislation; broadly, a tax-free transfer of property which would otherwise have given rise to income or capital gain.

royalty

A form of rent based on income from exploitation of natural resources or from the use of a patent, trademark or copyright.

rule of 78

(*colloq.*) Syn. for **sum-of-the-digits method.**

S

sale and leaseback

See **lease.**

sales

The periodical total proceeds from disposition of stock-in-trade or, by extension, from the rendering of services, net of returns and allowances. The terms "gross sales" and "net sales" are sometimes used to distinguish the sales aggregate before and after deduction of returns and allowances.

sales journal

The book of original entry in which sales are recorded.

salvage value

That portion of the residual value of an asset representing the value of parts reclaimed for future use after retirement of the asset. (Compare **scrap value.**)

sampling	*n.* The examination of a selection of items from a larger number of similar items, with the objective of judging the quality of the whole on the basis of the sample.
judgment sampling	Sampling in which the selection of items is determined subjectively.
random number sampling	Random sampling using a random number table.
random sampling	Sampling in which the selection of items is such that each item in the whole group has the same chance of being selected.
statistical sampling	Sampling in which the extent and interpretation of the selection is determined by statistical methods.
systematic sampling	Random sampling in which the selection begins at a randomly selected starting point with subsequent selections at every nth point.
scan	(*auditing*) To review data in order to locate significant items which may require further study. (Compare **scrutinize.**)
schedule	*n.* 1. A tabulated list of items. 2. A supplementary statement giving details of an item or items on a main statement.
scope paragraph	A paragraph in the audit report setting out the scope of the audit and the procedures followed in carrying out the engagement.
scrap value	That portion of the residual value of an asset representing the realizable value of metal or other material content after retirement of the asset. (Compare **salvage value.**)
scrutinize	(*auditing*) To review data searchingly in order to locate significant items which may require further study. (Compare **scan.**)
secondary distribution	The redistribution to the public of a significant block of securities of a corporation that have previously been distributed to the public. (Compare **primary distribution.**)
secondary issue	An issue of securities being offered in secondary distribution. (Compare **primary issue.**)
secret reserve	An amount by which the owners' equity in a business has been understated on the business' records as a result of an undervaluation or omission of assets or an overstatement of liabilities. This term does not represent a specific account bearing that name or disclosed in financial statements but rather a condition which exists.
secured creditor	See **creditor.**
secured liability	A debt or other obligation supported by certain assets upon which the creditor or person to whom the obligation is owed has a lien or which have been pledged to the creditor or person to whom the obligation is owed.
secured note	A promissory note evidencing a secured liability.
security	1. A bond or share certificate or other document evidencing

debt or ownership. 2. Property charged or pledged to secure the performance of a contract or the payment of a debt, e.g. land, buildings and plant in the case of mortgage bonds; accounts receivable, inventories or securities in the case of a bank loan.

segment margin
The contribution by a segment of a diversified company to the profitability of the company.

segmented information
Financial information related to the segments of a diversified company.

self-balancing ledger
A ledger in which the total of the accounts with debit balances should equal the total of the accounts with credit balances.

self-check digit
A digit forming part of an account or code number, normally the last digit of the number, which is mathematically derived from the other numbers of the code and is used to verify the accuracy of the code number.

self-insurance
See **insurance.**

sellers' market
A condition within an industry or geographic area where the demand for a product or service exceeds the supply; hence trading conditions favour the seller. (Compare **buyers' market.**)

selling expense
Expenses of an organization relating to the selling or marketing of its goods or services, as contrasted with expenses incurred for other specialized functions such as administration, financial, and manufacturing.

semi-variable cost
semi-variable expense
An indirect cost which varies with production or activity but not in direct proportion to the volume. (Compare **fixed cost; variable cost.**)

senior debt
Debt that has a higher priority of claims on assets and/or income than certain other debt. (Compare **subordinate debt.**)

senior security
Security that has a higher priority of claims on assets and/or income than certain other securities. (Compare **junior security.**)

sensitivity analysis
See **analysis.**

sequential access
See **access.**

serial bonds
See **bond** 1.

service bureau
Syn. for **data centre.**

service-output method
Syn. for **depreciation method—production method.**

settlement date
The date on which payment for goods or services rendered is made. The date on which stock exchange transactions are due for delivery and payment.

setup time
1. The length of time required to retool machines or change methods of production due to a change in product. 2. Syn. for **lead time.**

share	One of the equal parts into which each class of the capital stock of a limited company is divided.
acquired share	A share purchased by the issuing company and available for resale by that company. (Compare **cancelled share.**)
cancelled share	A share purchased by the issuing company and subsequently cancelled. (Compare **acquired share.**)
common share	A share of common stock. See **capital stock.**
cumulative share	A share of cumulative stock. See **capital stock.**
donated share	A share donated to the issuing company by a shareholder.
forfeited share	A share to which a subscriber has lost title because of nonpayment of a call.
non-cumulative share	A share of non-cumulative stock. See **capital stock.**
participating share	A share of participating stock. See **capital stock.**
preferred share	A share of preferred stock. See **capital stock.**
qualifying share	A share held by an individual to qualify as a director in the company.
reacquired share	(*colloq.*) Syn. for **acquired share.**
redeemable share	A share of redeemable stock. See **capital stock.**
repurchased share	(*colloq.*) Syn. for **acquired share.**
treasury shares	1. (*U.S.*) Syn. for **acquired shares.** 2. (*colloq.*) Authorized but unissued shares.
share capital	Syn. for **capital stock.**
authorized capital	The number and par value, if any, of shares of each class of capital stock that a company may issue in accordance with its instrument of incorporation.
contributed capital	Paid-up capital plus contributed surplus.
issued capital	The portion of authorized capital stock for which shares have been subscribed, allotted and entered in the share register, whether or not fully paid.
paid-up capital	1. That part of issued capital for which settlement has been received. 2. Under income tax legislation, the term has a special meaning.
stated capital	A term used in corporate legislation to designate the aggregate consideration received by a corporation on the issue of each class of share capital.
subscribed capital	Unissued capital for which offers have been received but not yet accepted by the directors.
unissued capital	The portion of authorized capital stock for which shares have not been issued.
share issue expense	Costs incurred when issuing shares, including legal fees, advertising, selling and printing costs.

share ledger **share register**	The record kept by a limited company of the ownership of its outstanding shares.
share right	A right granted to a shareholder on the occasion of a new issue of capital stock, which entitles him to purchase his pro rata share of the issue at a stated price and within a stated period of time. (Compare **stock purchase warrant.**)
share split	Syn. for **stock split.**
shareholder	The legal owner of shares of a limited company.
shareholder of record	A shareholder in whose name shares are registered in the books of a limited company.
shareholders' deficiency	The excess of the book value of liabilities of a limited company over the book value of its assets; negative shareholders' equity.
shareholders' equity	The interest of the shareholders in the net assets of a limited company.
shipping order	A form conveying instructions for the shipment of specified goods.
short position	The condition of a seller who is obliged to deliver securities or commodities to a broker; such seller is said to be ''short'' those securities or commodities in the broker's accounts. (Compare **long position.**)
short sale	The sale of a security or commodity not owned by the seller in the hope that the security or commodity can subsequently be purchased before the settlement date at a lower price. See also **short position.**
short-form report	An audit report the substance of which contains only two elements: a statement of the scope of the examination and an opinion on the financial statements. (Compare **long-form report.**)
short-term liability	Syn. for **current liability.**
shutdown cost	1. Those fixed costs which continue to be incurred after production has ceased. 2. The costs of closing down a particular production facility.
sight draft	A bill of exchange payable on sight, i.e. on demand or presentation, but with respect to which three days of grace are allowed for payment.
signing officer	1. An officer authorized to sign certain documents on behalf of an organization. 2. In a restricted sense, the individual who signs cheques or bills of exchange on behalf of an organization.
single entry bookkeeping	A form of bookkeeping in which only cash books and/or personal accounts are maintained in simple or notation form without a self-balancing ledger. (Compare **double entry bookkeeping.**)
single proprietorship	Syn. for **sole proprietorship.**

single-step income statement	That form of income statement in which all items of revenue are grouped and extended in one total, as are all items of expense, the latter being deducted from the former to arrive at a single figure of net income. (Compare **multi-step income statement.**)
sinking fund	A pool of cash and investments, usually built up systematically, earmarked to provide resources for the redemption of debt or capital stock.
sinking fund bonds	See **bond** 1.
sinking fund method	See **depreciation method.**
sinking fund reserve	A portion of retained earnings appropriated for the purposes of a sinking fund.
social accounting	The identification, measurement and reporting of social costs and benefits of human activity.
social costs	The loss to society resulting from action or inaction in particular circumstances. Such costs are often not readily measurable in monetary terms.
software	The programming aids, such as compilers, sort and report programs, and generators, which extend the capabilities of and simplify the use of the computer, as well as certain operating systems and other control programs. (Compare **hardware.**)
sole proprietorship	An unincorporated business wholly owned by one person.
solvency	The ability of an individual or corporation to pay its debts as they become due. (Compare **liquidity.**)
source and application of funds, statement of	See **statement of source and application of funds.**
source document	The original record or evidence of a transaction.
specific identification	See **cost allocation methods.**
spot check	A term loosely used with reference to audit sampling techniques.
stale-dated cheque	See **cheque.**
standard cost	The projected cost of an activity, operation, process or item of product, established as a basis for control and reporting.
standard cost system standard costing	See **cost accounting method.**
standard hours	The number of hours set as the standard for producing a particular unit or providing a particular service.
stand-by charges	Charges incurred for the right of having resources such as equipment or services available at short notice.
standing order	An order issued as authority for the production or purchase of goods or services, as need or opportunity arise, usually limited by a stated maximum.

start-up costs	The aggregate of the costs, excluding acquisition costs, incurred to bring a new unit into production.
stated capital	See **share capital.**
stated value	1. The amount at which the capital stock of a limited company is carried in the accounts; in the case of par value shares, the par value; and in the case of no par value shares, the amount determined by resolution of the board of directors. 2. Syn. for **book value** 1.
statement	1. A transcript of a personal account. 2. Any document setting forth financial data in a more or less formal arrangement. See **financial statement.**
statement, cash	Syn. for **statement of receipts and disbursements.**
statement, cash flow	A financial statement showing the net effect of operations and other types of transactions for a period on the cash position. It is similar to the statement of source and application of funds except that it also takes into account changes in current assets and liabilities, other than cash. (Compare **statement of receipts and disbursements.**)
statement, common-size	A financial statement in which the components are expressed as a percent of a specific item included in the statement; in the case of the balance sheet, the total assets and the total liabilities and owners' equities respectively, and in the case of the income statement, the net sales.
statement, income	A financial statement summarizing the items of revenue, income, expenses and losses for a stated period. (Compare **statement of revenue and expenditure.**)
statement, manufacturing	A financial statement showing particulars of the cost of the goods manufactured.
statement, operating	Syn. for **statement, income.**
statement of account	See **statement** 1.
statement of affairs	A statement of assets and liabilities prepared in the case of actual or impending bankruptcy or insolvency, showing the effects of immediate liquidation, and the proposed distribution of the proceeds having regard to the rights of the various classes of creditors and owners.
statement of changes in financial position	A financial statement showing, for a stated period, how the activities of the enterprise have been financed, including the extent to which funds have been generated from operations, how the financial resources have been used and the effects of these activities on the funds of the enterprise.
statement of changes in net assets	A statement of changes in financial position adapted for investment companies. The details provided include a reconciliation of the net assets at the beginning and end of the period with emphasis on transactions and fluctuations in market value affecting the investment portfolio.

statement of charge and discharge A financial statement as to capital and income, drawn up by an executor or administrator to account for receipts and dispositions of cash and/or other assets in an estate or trust.

statement of contributed surplus A financial statement summarizing the changes in contributed surplus for a stated period.

statement of earnings Syn. for **statement, income.**

statement of financial position Syn. for **balance sheet.**

statement of income See **statement, income.**

statement of material facts Under securities legislation, a document filed by a corporation with a securities commission relating to a proposed primary distribution of securities exempt from prospectus requirements. It contains information concerning the securities, circumstances relating to their offering, names of the corporation's officers and directors, financial data and other pertinent facts.

statement of profit and loss Syn. for **statement, income.**

statement of realization and liquidation A financial statement drawn up by a trustee or liquidator to account for the winding-up of a business, showing the amounts realized on disposition of the assets and the amounts disbursed to liquidate the liabilities.

statement of receipts and disbursements A financial statement showing the opening and closing balances of cash on hand and in bank and summarizing the cash receipts and disbursements for a stated period. (Compare **statement, cash flow.**)

statement of retained earnings A financial statement summarizing the changes in retained earnings for a stated period.

statement of revenue and expenditure A financial statement summarizing the items of revenue and expenditure for a stated period. It is most often used by governmental and other non-profit organizations. (Compare **statement, income.**)

statement of revenue and expense Syn. for **statement, income.**

statement of source and application of funds A statement of changes in financial position which takes into account only those activities which have an effect on working capital.

statistical sampling See **sampling.**

statutory amalgamation See **business combination.**

statutory audit See **audit.**

stock	1. Syn. for **capital stock**. 2. Syn. for **inventory** 2.
stock dividend	See **dividend** 1.
stock-in-trade	Syn. for **inventory** 2.
stock option	A right granted by a limited company to purchase a specified number of shares of the company's capital stock at a stated price within a stated period of time.
stock purchase warrant	A certificate giving the owner of preferred shares or bonds of a limited company the right to purchase a specified number of shares of the company's capital stock at a stated price within a stated period of time. (Compare **share right**.)
stock split	Increase in the number of shares of a class of capital stock, with no change in the total dollar amount of the class, but with a converse reduction in the par or stated value of the shares. This is achieved by replacing a specified number of new shares for one old share. (Compare **consolidation** (of shares).)
stockholder	Syn. for **shareholder**.
stop payment	An order by the drawer of a cheque to the bank on which it is drawn not to pay the cheque.
stores	Direct or indirect materials.
straight-line method	See **depreciation method**.
street security	(*colloq.*) Syn. for **bearer security**.
subordinate debt	Debt that has a lower priority of claims on assets and/or income than certain other debt. (Compare **senior debt**.)
subscribed capital	See **share capital**.
subscription	1. A contract with a publisher providing for the delivery by the publisher of a periodical publication for a stated length of time. 2. An agreement to purchase shares of a limited company. 3. Syn. for **pledge**.
subsequent event	An event of material financial consequence that affects an accounting entity and occurs between the date of the financial statements and the date of their issuance.
subsidiary company	A corporation in which another corporation owns a majority of the shares carrying the right to elect at least a majority of the members of the board of directors. (Compare **parent company**.)
subsidiary ledger	A ledger in which individual accounts of the same type are kept (e.g. customers' accounts); the aggregate of these accounts is maintained in a control account in the general ledger.
sum-of-the-digits method	A method of allocating unearned income on instalment contracts to accounting periods. The unearned income is allocated to the individual periods on a reducing basis by multiplying it by a fraction in which the numerator is the number of periods remaining + 1 and the denominator is the sum of the numbers representing the periods. For a note repayable in equal instalments over twelve months, the

denominator is 78, and the numerator for the first month is 12, for the second month 11, and so on.

sum-of-the-years'-digits method
See **depreciation method.**

sunk cost
A cost associated with an irreversible past decision.

supplementary earnings per share
(*U.S.*) See **earnings per share.**

supplies
Materials which are consumed in the operations of a business but do not become part of the physical content of any finished product.

surplus
The excess of net assets over stated value of the issued shares of a limited company; the excess of assets over liabilities of a non-profit organization.

capital surplus
1. The statutory designation under certain corporations legislation to describe retained earnings appropriated in connection with the redemption of preferred shares under certain circumstances. See **reserve.** 2. (*obs.*) Premium on shares issued. See **contributed surplus** 1. 3. (*obs.*) Accumulated capital gains; a portion of retained earnings.

contributed surplus
1. Surplus contributed by shareholders, being the premium received on the issue of par value shares, the portion of proceeds of issue of no par value shares that has been allocated to surplus, the proceeds of sale of donated shares, profit on forfeited shares, credits resulting from redemption or conversion of shares at less than the amount set up as share capital, or any other contributions in excess of stated value of shares made by shareholders as such. 2. Capital donations from sources other than shareholders.

distributable surplus
The statutory designation under certain corporations legislation to describe the portion of the proceeds of the issue of shares without par value not allocated to share capital.

donated surplus
The value of gifts of assets to the corporation from shareholders or others; a form of **contributed surplus.**

earned surplus
(*obs.*) Syn. for **retained earnings.**

paid-in surplus
Syn. for **contributed surplus.**

retained earnings
The accumulated balance of income less losses of a corporation, after taking into account dividends and other appropriate charges or credits.

appropriated retained earnings
Retained earnings which have been transferred to a reserve. See **reserve.**

deficit
Any accumulated negative balance of retained earnings.

unappropriated retained earnings
Retained earnings which have not been transferred to a reserve.

suspense account	An account to which an entry for a transaction is posted until ultimate disposition is determined, e.g. receipt of cash from an unidentified source. (Compare **clearing account.**)
systematic sampling	See **sampling.**
systems design	The specification of an organizational set-up and of the procedures and methods to be used in carrying out an activity.

T

T-account	A basic form of account which consists of only three parts: a title, a left side for debits and a right side for credits; so called because it resembles a T.
takeover bid	A bid to purchase shares of a limited company with a view to gaining control.
tangible asset	An asset that is not an intangible asset.
tax allocation	The process of apportioning income taxes within or among accounting periods.
interperiod tax allocation	The process of apportioning income taxes among periods. (Compare **intraperiod tax allocation; taxes payable basis.**)
accrual method	A method of applying the tax allocation basis where the amount by which the current tax provision differs from the amount of taxes currently payable is considered to reflect the recognition in the current period of taxes expected to be recoverable or payable in a future period. Adjustments are made to accumulated amounts to reflect changes in tax rates.
deferral method	A method of applying the tax allocation basis where the amount by which the current tax provision differs from the amount of taxes currently payable is considered to represent the deferment to future periods of a benefit obtained or expenditure currently incurred. Adjustments are not made to accumulated amounts to reflect changes in tax rates.
net-of-tax method	A method of applying the tax allocation basis where the tax effects of timing differences are reflected by adjustments of the valuation of the assets and liabilities involved and the related revenues and expenses.
intraperiod tax allocation	The process of apportioning income tax expense applicable to a given period between income before extraordinary items and extraordinary items, and of associating with items included in retained earnings the income tax effects of such items. (Compare **interperiod tax allocation.**)
tax avoidance	The minimization of the impact of taxation by taking advantage of all allowances and benefits that the law provides. (Compare **tax evasion.**)
tax credit	See **deferred income taxes.**
tax debit	See **deferred income taxes.**

tax equity	A term in income tax legislation; broadly, the net assets of a corporation.
tax evasion	The willful attempt to escape the impact of taxation through subterfuge or other infraction of the law. (Compare **tax avoidance.**)
tax haven	(*colloq.*) A political jurisdiction that levies significantly lower taxes than would otherwise be payable in other jursidictions on similar income.
tax lien	An encumbrance placed upon a taxpayer's property as security for unpaid taxes.
tax planning	The arrangements of the affairs of an individual or an enterprise with a view to tax avoidance.
tax roll	A record of persons subject to taxation and of taxes levied.
tax shelter **tax shield**	(*colloq.*) A situation in which income that would otherwise be taxable is offset by allowable expenses which do not affect the flow of working capital.
taxable income	Income for a period, subject to taxation, as computed in accordance with income tax legislation. (Compare **accounting income.**)
taxes payable basis	A basis used in accounting for corporate income taxes where there are timing differences between accounting income and taxable income. The charge for income taxes is the estimated amount that will actually be levied for the period. (Compare **tax allocation—interperiod tax allocation.**)
term loan	A loan for a stipulated period of time. (Compare **demand loan.**)
test	*n.* Syn. for **sampling.**
test audit	See **audit.**
testamentary trust	See **trust.**
thin capitalization	A state of having a high debt to equity ratio. Under income tax legislation, the term has a special meaning.
tickler file	A record of items maintained to call attention to each item at the proper time for it to be dealt with.
time deposit	A deposit in a bank or other financial institution for a specific minimum period of time. (Compare **demand deposit.**)
timing differences	Differences between accounting income and taxable income which arise when items of revenue and expense are included in the computation of accounting income in one period but are included in the computation of taxable income in another period. (Compare **permanent differences.**)
trace	*v.* (*auditing*) To follow a business transaction through the various phases in the business records.
trade acceptance	A bill of exchange given in respect of goods or services supplied to the acceptor.

trade account payable	A debt for goods or services purchased in the ordinary course of business. See also **account payable.**
trade account receivable	An amount claimed against a customer for goods or services sold to him in the ordinary course of business. See also **account receivable.**
trade discount	See **discount** *n.* 1.
trademark	An intangible asset consisting of a word, symbol or mark used to identify goods or services with their producer.
transfer agent	An agent of a corporation responsible for the issue, recording and cancellation of its bond or share certificates. (Compare **registrar.**)
transfer price	The price charged by one segment of an enterprise for a product or service which it provides to another segment of the enterprise.
translation of foreign currency	The process of expressing financial statements derived from a set of accounts maintained in the currency of one country in terms of the currency of another country, or of expressing monetary items which are stated in one currency in equivalent terms of another currency. (Compare **conversion of foreign currency.**)
treasury bill	A short-term government security issued at a discount in lieu of interest.
treasury shares	See **share.**
trial balance	A list of all account balances in a ledger, usually showing the account numbers or names, prepared to ascertain whether the ledger is in balance.
trust	A relationship between two persons by virtue of which one of them (the trustee) holds property for the benefit of, and stands in a fudiciary relationship to, the other (the beneficiary).
inter-vivos trust	A trust created and coming into existence during the lifetime of the person at whose instance it has been created (the settlor). (Compare **testamentary trust.**)
testamentary trust	A trust created upon the death of a person through his will. (Compare **inter-vivos trust.**)
trust deed **trust indenture**	1. An instrument whereby a trust of property is declared. 2. An instrument by which title to property is conveyed to a trustee as security for a debt. It describes the rights and obligations of the borrower, creditors and the trustee while the debt remains outstanding.
trustee	A person who holds title to property for the benefit of another.
trustee in bankruptcy	A person appointed by the court to administer the estate of a bankrupt and distribute available assets to creditors.
trust fund	Property (especially cash and securities) which has been

conveyed or assigned to a trustee to be administered as directed.

turnover

1. A measure of business activity relating to current assets, showing the number of times assets of a given class have been liquidated and replaced by other assets of the same class within a given period of time. 2. (*Br.*) Sales.

U

unappropriated retained earnings

See **surplus—retained earnings.**

undepreciated cost

That portion of cost yet to be depreciated.

underabsorb

v. To charge to production estimated overhead which is less than actual overhead. (Compare **overabsorb.**)

underabsorbed burden
underapplied burden

See **overhead.**

underwriter

1. A person who issues an insurance contract. 2. A term in corporations legislation; broadly, a person who subscribes for part or all of any issue of securities with a view to reselling them.

underwriting commission

Commission payable to an underwriter of an issue of securities.

undistributed income

A term in income tax legislation; broadly, retained earnings of a corporation.

unearned income
unearned revenue

Income or revenue received or receivable but not yet earned.

unexpired cost

The portion of an expenditure whose benefit has not been exhausted. (Compare **expired cost.**)

unfunded pension plan

See **pension plan.**

uniform code of accounts

A system of accounts prescribing standardized accounting treatment and classification for use by organizations of a given type.

unincorporated business

A business organization which is not a legal entity separate from its owners or members.

unissued capital

See **share capital.**

unit

1. One of the equal parts into which the ownership of a mutual fund or real estate investment trust is divided. 2. A package of two or more securities of different classes of a corporation offered for sale.

unit benefit pension plan

Syn. for **pension plan—benefit based pension plan.**

unit cost

The cost of a unit of product or service, found by dividing the total applied costs for a given period or for a given operation by the number of units produced in that period or operation.

unit depreciation	See **depreciation unit.**
unlisted	Relating to securities which are traded but not listed on an established stock exchange. See also **over-the-counter.**
unpaid dividend	See **dividend** 1.
unqualified opinion	See **auditor's opinion.**
unsecured account	An account receivable or payable, for which no collateral has been given.
useful life	Syn. for **economic life.**

V

value added tax (VAT)	A tax levied at each stage in the production and distribution chain on the basis of the value that is added to the goods or services passing through that stage.
variable budget	Syn. for **budget—flexible budget.**
variable cost **variable expense**	A cost that varies directly with the volume of production or activity. (Compare **fixed cost; semi-variable cost.**)
variance	1. The difference between budgeted or expected performance and actual performance. 2. (*standard costing*) The difference between actual and standard for a cost element, e.g. material price variance, material quantity variance, labour price variance.
efficiency variance	A term applied to quantity variance in some circumstances.
price variance	The difference between the standard cost of direct materials and/or labour and the actual cost, resulting from changes in the input prices.
quantity variance	The difference between the standard cost of direct materials and/or labour and the actual cost, resulting from changes in the input quantities.
rate variance	A term sometimes applied to labour price variance.
venture accounting	The method of accounting for a specific business undertaking, in which all costs and revenues are carried forward as a net figure in the balance sheet of the venturer and the results are not determined until the venture is completed.
verification	(*auditing*) The process of establishing the validity of accuracy of entries, records or statements.
vertical analysis	See **ratio analysis.**
vertical business combination	See **business combination.**
vertical integration	The extension of activity by an organization into businesses directly related to the production or distribution of the organization's end products. Although products may be sold to

others at various stages, a substantial proportion of the output at each stage is devoted to the production of the end products. (Compare **horizontal integration.**)

vesting
The accrual to an employee of rights under a pension plan, arising from employer contributions.

volume discount
See **discount** *n.* 1.

voting trust
An agreement among security holders of a corporation whereby their votes are to be cast by a trustee in the interests of the group.

vouch
To verify by examination of supporting documents.

voucher
Any evidence of a documentary nature in support of an accounting entry.

voucher register
A book of original entry for expenditures which combines the functions of a cash disbursements book and a subsidiary record of vouchers payable.

voucher system
A system for recording expenditures based on the use of a voucher register.

voyage accounting
The application of venture accounting to individual maritime voyages.

W

warehouse receipt
Documentary evidence issued by the operator of a public warehouse that goods are being held in storage on behalf of their owner.

warranty
n. A written statement promising remedial action on the part of the vendor if defects are found in goods sold during a stated period. (Compare **guarantee** 1.)

warranty repairs
Repairs to goods sold under warranty, the expense being borne by the vendor or manufacturer.

wasting assets
Natural resources which are subject to depletion through the process of extraction or use, e.g. standing timber and mineral deposits.

watered stock
(*colloq.*) Capital stock issued for consideration which is worth less than the stated value of the stock.

wear and tear
Physical deterioration of a capital asset through use or exposure to the elements.

wholesale price index
See **price index.**

window-dressing
(*colloq.*) A generic term applied to methods of improperly enhancing the picture shown by financial statements.

wind-up
winding-up
To bring to an end, such as the life of a corporation. The latter is accomplished either by (1) following the winding-up

provisions of applicable statutes, (2) surrendering the charter or (3) following banrkuptcy proceedings; the method used depends on the state of the affairs of the corporation.

withholding tax
A tax deduction at source.

working capital
The excess of current assets over current liabilities.

working capital ratio
Syn. for **ratio analysis—current ratio.**

working papers
Schedules, transcripts, analyses, confirmations, notes and other memoranda prepared and accumulated by an accountant or auditor in the performance of his duties.

work in process
work in progress
Partly-finished goods or contracts which are in the process of manufacture or completion.

work order
Written instructions for the execution of specified work usually with specifications for the materials to be issued and the labour to be employed.

write down
v. To record an unrealized decrease in the value of an asset, or a reduction in the amount of liability without equivalent consideration.

write off
v. To transfer to income or surplus all or a portion of the balance in an asset or liability account.

write up
v. 1. To record an unrealized increase in the value of an asset. 2. (*colloq.*) To enter transactions in the books of account.

Y

year-end audit
See **audit.**

yield
Syn. for **effective rate.**

yield to maturity
The effective rate of return to be realized on a bond or debenture assuming it is held to maturity. The rate is determined by comparing the expected total flow of funds (interest and principal) to the price.

Z

zero-based budgeting
(Used chiefly in government.) A management system whereby all programs are re-evaluated each time a new budget is formulated. The benefits associated with different levels of expenditures for a particular objective are identified in terms of progress towards meeting that objective.